CORPORATE & COMMERCIAL LAW SERIES

LAW OF RESTITUTION

Andrew Tettenborn, MA, LLB, Barrister
Fellow of Pembroke College and
Lecturer in Law at the
University of Cambridge

Cavendish
Publishing
Limited

First published in Great Britain 1993 by Cavendish Publishing Limited, 23A Countess Road, London NW5 2XH.

Telephone: 071–485 0303   Facsimile: 071–485 0304

© Tettenborn, A 1993

British Library Cataloguing in Publication Data

Tettenborn, A M
Law of Restitution
I Title
344.20777

ISBN 1-874241-88-0

Printed and bound in Great Britain

CONTENTS

CONTENTS

CONTENTS

CONTENTS

CONTENTS

TABLE OF STATUTES

TABLE OF CASES

CHAPTER 1

THE CONCEPT OF RESTITUTION

1 RESTITUTION AND UNJUSTIFIED ENRICHMENT

If you are lucky, you may end to-day richer than you started it. You **1-01** may be paid a sum of money or be given a car: someone else may discharge a debt of yours, or render you a service such as repairing your bicycle. If you have a piece of commercial information, you may turn it to your advantage and make a large sum of money out of it. Now, in the majority of such cases the law has nothing to say about this. Gains, like losses, *prima facie* lie where they fall. If I make you a gift of £100 or a car, that is your good luck: if I pay you £1,000 for goods supplied, or clean your windows because I have contracted to do so, you are merely receiving what is due to you. That is what economic life is about.

But some cases are different. With some gains, you cannot simply pre-empt the issue by putting them down to good luck, or business, or the nature of things, or the important presumption running through English law that gifts are irrevocable. For example, when I gave you £100, I might have forgotten that I had already transferred £100 to your account last week, and thus was making the same gift twice: I might equally have only done so because I thought I was richer than I was. I may have cleaned your windows, not from any feeling of benevolence or because I intended to benefit you, but for some entirely different reason. You might have asked me to do so pending the outcome of negotiations for a long-term window-cleaning contract between us: or I might have mistaken your house for that of your neighbour, whose windows I had agreed to clean. Again, take the payment of £1,000. Although this was made for goods supplied, this is not the end of the story: I may have refused to accept the goods concerned; it may turn out that you only delivered part of them, or that what you did deliver was were substandard; and so on.

This is what the law of restitution is about. More formally, restitution **1-02** is the response of the law to enrichment which it regards as unjustified: that is, that area of the law which:

    (1) decides which of your gains should be left to stand, and which should be regarded as unjustified and reversed or redistributed; and

(2)   in the latter case, where you are not allowed to keep your gain, determines

(a)   who should be given a remedy against you; and

(b)   what form that remedy should take.

2   THE REQUIREMENTS OF UNJUSTIFIED ENRICHMENT[1]

1-03   In order to obtain restitution for unjustified enrichment, the plaintiff has on principle to show three things:

(a)   a gain by the defendant, i.e. enrichment;

(b)   that that gain is unjustified; and

(c)   that it was made at his expense – more accurately, that he in particular has title to sue to reverse it. This chapter will now proceed to elucidate these three vital concepts.

Gain by the defendant

1-04   Restitution is about recovery for gains. Without a gain of some sort made by the person from whom restitution is sought, there can be no enrichment at all, justified or otherwise, and hence no restitution. But in this part of the law, 'gain' is a very wide term. It includes, it is suggested, anything amounting to a benefit which has, or might have, money value to the person to whom it accrues. (True, this is an expansive definition, and to that extent is controversial[2]: nevertheless, it is submitted that clarity of thought is best served by casting the net as wide as possible, while always remembering that not all benefits engender restitutionary claims and that one can, at a later stage suitably restrict the circumstances in which recovery will be allowed.)

I therefore gain if I receive money, or property, or the use of money or property, or if you improve an existing asset of mine. I gain from work you do on my property, such as building work, whether or not I asked you to do it, and whether or not you thereby increase its market value. I gain from payment of or discharge of my debts or other charges binding me or my property; and indeed from any service rendered to, or benefiting me.

---

1   'Unjustified enrichment' and 'unjust enrichment' are used virtually synonymously in this book. Detailed discussion of what is meant by these terms will be found later on in this chapter.

2   *Cf* Beatson, *The Use and Abuse of Unjust Enrichment,* Chapter 2; Burrows, *The Law of Restitution,* pp.8-9.

Yet again, the concept of 'gain' also includes, where appropriate, benefits rendered, not to me myself, but to others on my orders: if you wrongly think you owe me £100 but at my request pay it to a third party, this remains a gain in my hands[3].

There are three further important points about gain which fall to be made at this stage.

The concept of 'gain': subjective or objective?

It is submitted that the concept of gain, like its companion loss, is best understood objectively. Just as in the law of tort you can claim the value of a chair you have lost whether or not you ever sat in it or missed it when it had gone, so conversely in restitution: something may be a gain to you, even though you do not want it and do not in fact benefit from it. So, for example, you gain if you receive services for which there is a market value, independently of whether those services produce any end-product: if I engage you to research and write a book for me, the research work you do is a gain to me[4].

1-05

This is not to deny, of course, that there may well be good reasons for not making you pay for such 'gains'. For example, in *B.P. (Exploration) Ltd. v. Hunt*[5] s.1(3) of the Law Reform (Frustrated Contracts) Act 1943, which requires a party to a frustrated contract in certain cases to pay for 'valuable benefits' received, was construed as referring, in the case of services where an 'end-product' was contemplated, merely to the value of that 'end-product'. But that result did not (it is submitted) turn on any definitional point: it was merely an understandable refusal to make someone pay for services from which in fact he got no benefit whatever. This point is important. Take the case of unrequested and unbeneficial services; for example, I clean your windows, which you yourself preferred to keep dirty and would never have bothered to have cleaned yourself. Normally there is no recovery in cases like this: however meritorious I may be, I am normally sent empty away on the very sensible ground that the state has no business to make you pay for goods or services you did not ask for, accept or agree to buy[6]. But even here, there are exceptional cases where recovery ought to be allowed. Arguably, for instance, if you abandon your cat and out of humanity I feed it, I should be able to claim from you[7]. The difficulty is, of course,

1-06

---

3   It may also be a gain to the third party, though it is unlikely that restitution would be granted against him. See para. 15-08 below.

4   *Planché v. Colbum* (1831) 8 Bing 14.

5   [1982] 1 All E.R. 925.

6   As it will not in contract: *Felthouse v. Bindley* (1862) 11 CB(NS) 869, aff'd (1863) 7 L.T. 835.

7   *Cf Great Northern Ry v. Swaffield* (1874) 9 Ex. 132, and para. 8-10 below.

that if we said that such services could not by definition amount to a benefit at all, there would be no restitutionary peg on which to hang this kind of exceptional, but useful, head of recovery.

Measuring the gain

1-07   The second difficulty concerns the value of a gain. It is submitted that, for clarity of thought, the amount of a gain should always fall to be reckoned as its market price, and that it should be taken at the time it was received by the defendant. Thus, suppose I paint your house by mistake, for which the going rate is £1,000; suppose further that you were about to paint it yourself, but for the unusually advantageous price of £600. Your gain (it is suggested) is £1,000, even though it is arguable that my recovery ought to be only £600.

Again, on the question of timing, it is the time of receipt that ought to matter rather than any other date (such as the time when restitution is requested, or when proceedings are taken to obtain it). Thus if I pay you £1,000 which I later reclaim after the contract under which it was paid has been frustrated, no account is taken as a matter of the law of restitution of the fact that you have had the use of the money: your gain remains £1,000[8]. Conversely, if I pay you £1,000 by mistake and you some days later spend £800 as a result, your gain is still £1,000, no more, no less.

Of course this does not mean that my *claim* is necessarily for the amount of your gain. In the first case your use of the money can be partly offset by an award of statutory interest[9]: in the second, if you had spent the £800 in all innocence, you would have a defence of change of position except as to £200[10]. Indeed, there are cases where the plaintiff's recovery is specifically limited to the amount of the gain remaining in the defendant's hands. Tracing claims are the best example. If my trustee steals trust shares, sells them for £1,000 and gives you the proceeds, whereupon you spend £400, my tracing claim against you is limited to £600 (whatever other claims I may have against you for the rest). But none of these affects the amount of the gain: they merely reflect the fact that it is (rightly) more difficult to obtain restitutionary recovery from one who does not still have the assets gained than from one who does.

Gains not all treated similarly

1-08   While all the various forms of gain outlined above may figure in the law of unjust enrichment, this does not mean that anyone with a

---

[8]   *B.P. (Exploration) v. Hunt* [1982] 1 All E.R. 925.

[9]   Under s. 35A of the Supreme Court Act 1981: *B.P. (Exploration) v. Hunt* [1982] 1 All E.R. 925.

[10] See para. 15-09 ff below.

restitution claim can necessarily recover all of them from the particular defendant concerned. The principle of unjustified enrichment is simply not that abstract: it regards it as perfectly acceptable that certain heads of restitutionary recovery should encompass some forms of gain, but not others.

For instance, if you wrongfully exploit my land, it seems I can recover 'positive' profits made by you (e.g. if you charge the public for admission), but not 'negative' profits (e.g. you save yourself the cost of leasing other land[11]). Nor should this necessarily be surprising: there may well be good reasons for distinguishing between forms of gain, just as in the law of tort it has never caused undue concern that different torts should exist in order to compensate different kinds of loss.

A gain which is 'unjustified'

Assuming a gain by the defendant, the vital question - with which, in one shape or another, the majority of this book will be taken up - is whether it is 'unjustified', so as to call for action to reverse it. At this stage, however, a few general observations are in order.   **1-09**

First, there is an obvious point: 'unjustified' means more than simply 'unfair' or 'unjust' in the wide sense. There is no more a right to recover gains from someone else whenever it is fair and reasonable, than there is a right of recovery in tort merely on the ground that one has suffered a loss and that it is fair and reasonable that someone else should pay for it. Thus, if I want to take a given gain from you, I must show some specifically legal ground to attack it. True, there are a good many of these. You may have profited from wrongfully selling my car, or I may have paid you £100 by mistake, or done work for you under a contract which for some reason turned out not to be effective. But it is up to the law to define what these situations are: to lay down the circumstances that will, for these purposes, render a gain 'unjustified' and hence open to a claim for restitution.

Secondly, 'justification' is a highly flexible concept. Although there is a common thread running through all unjustified enrichment claims - the need for a gain by the defendant, some reason for the law to regard that gain as unjustified, and some title in the plaintiff to claim it from him - the rules do vary as between particular heads of restitutionary recovery as to what factors will make a given gain 'unjustified', or conversely make it acceptable for the defendant to be allowed to hold on to it.   **1-10**

For example, in some cases the fact that the defendant had no chance of rejecting the gain will prevent any claim arising in respect of it: the reasoning being that I can hardly be said to act unjustifiably if I insist on

---

[11] If, at least, the decision in *Phillips v. Homfray* (1883) 24 Ch. D. 439 is correct.

holding on to a benefit which I received willy-nilly and cannot readily turn into money so as to find the means to pay for it[12]. Thus if you paint the outside of my house while I am away because you have mistaken it for my neighbour's which you have agreed to paint, you have no claim against me[13]. On the other hand, this is not always so. If you buy a picture which has been stolen from me and, thinking that it is yours, have it cleaned, then you are entitled, when I claim the picture back, to an allowance for your improvements[14]: in this case the law does regard it as unjustified for me to recover a better picture from you than I lost. Take another example. Normally the fact that the defendant has positively refused a benefit will bar any claim in respect of it: if the plaintiff goes ahead and confers it anyway, he is regarded as having made a gift of it which the defendant is justified in keeping[15]. But not always: a salvage claim, for instance, may lie even in respect of services which have been refused[16].

The plaintiff's title to claim: enrichment 'at the plaintiff's expense'

1-11   The third requirement for a claim in unjustified enrichment is a good deal more enigmatic. It is normally formulated as follows: to give rise to a claim, the defendant's gain must not only be unjustified, but it must have been made 'at the expense of the plaintiff'.

The essential thinking behind this is not difficult. Assume I wrongly think I owe you £1,000. In order to save trouble, I tell X, a friend of mine who happens to owe me £1,000, that I have this debt to you, and ask him to pay you directly. X does so. Now, if X were to sue you for the return of the £1,000, he would lose, despite the fact that your enrichment is clearly unjustified (you have got £1,000 in respect of a bogus debt), and despite the fact that he paid under a mistake (had he and I known the true facts the payment would never have been made). The reason is that any enrichment you have gained has been at my expense, not X's: I am the person to sue, not X.

So far so good. Nevertheless, it is suggested that the phrase 'at the plaintiff's expense' is a difficult and deceptive one in this connection, since (if one gives the word 'expense' its normal meaning) it is both too narrow and too wide.

---

[12] See below, Chapter 14.

[13] See below, para. 3-18.

[14] Now under s. 6 of the Torts (Interference with Goods) Act 1977: previously at common law (*Greenwood v. Bennett* [1973] Q.B. 195).

[15] See below, para. 15-04.

[16] *The Kangaroo* [1918] P. 327; below, para. 8-13 ff.

Too narrow

It is too narrow, because 'expense' suggests the necessity of either a **1-12** direct transfer from the plaintiff to the defendant, or at the very least a corresponding impoverishment in the plaintiff. Now, this will indeed be so in many cases. A direct payment is one clear instance, and the above example is another (since I am impoverished because my friend no longer owes me £1,000, whereas my friend is not: his debt to me is discharged by the payment to you, which means he is in no worse a position).

But not always. Take the case of the trustee who profits from his office, or the agent who takes a bribe. In both cases there is clear authority that the gain must be given up to the beneficiary or principal, whether or not there is any evidence that the latter has suffered loss or would, but for the fiduciary's wrongdoing, have received the gain concerned[17]. Again, assume that, while you are away, I unlawfully borrow your car and use it as a minicab. Even though you have suffered no loss, and had no intention to use or profit from the car while away (you were happy for it to stagnate in your garage), I have to account to you for the money I made[18]. Any definition of the phrase 'at the plaintiff's expense' must be able to accommodate these situations.

Too wide

The phrase 'at the plaintiff's expense' is also too wide, since it is **1-13** possible to imagine situations where the defendant has gained, that gain is unjustified, and the plaintiff has lost as a result, but nevertheless the plaintiff still fails because the gain was not at his expense.

Suppose X wrongly believes he owns Blackacre, which actually belongs to me, and I encourage him in that belief. Suppose further that X engages you, a builder, to develop Blackacre, thus greatly increasing its value. You do so, but then X fails to pay you. There is no doubt that in these circumstances I am unjustified in holding on to the increased value of Blackacre: nevertheless, if you sue me for restitution, you will fail. You looked for payment to X, not me: the proper plaintiff is not you but X, the person who commissioned the work in the first place[19].

The real issue: who should have title to sue?

The answer is, it is suggested, to the problem of enrichment 'at the **1-14** plaintiff's expense' is that this requirement actually represents a much

---

[17] See below, para. 11-17 ff.

[18] *Cf Strand Electric v. Brisford Entertainments* [1952] 2 Q.B. 246, and para. 11-07 below.

[19] On the principle in *Unity Joint Stock Banking Co. v. King* (1858) 25 Beav. 72: below, para. 3-20.

more general rule: *a plaintiff cannot sue to reverse unjustified enrichment unless, in the circumstances, the law gives him title to sue.* The question therefore becomes simply this: given that the defendant has been enriched, and unjustifiably so, in what circumstances will a given plaintiff have *locus standi* to recover that enrichment from him? The answer can be expressed in two propositions: one positive, one negative.

The positive proposition, which explains why the traditional definition is too narrow, is that direct transfer and/or corresponding impoverishment is one way of establishing title to sue, but not the only one. There are at least three others.

(1) Relationships

1-15   A right to restitution may arise out of a given relationship, in which case that relationship will also govern who has title to sue. An example is trustee and beneficiary: if a trustee profits from his trust, the person who can claim that profit is his beneficiary. Another is principal and agent: the agent who takes a bribe must pay it over to his principal.

(2) Wrongs

1-16   Another potential source of restitutionary recovery is the commission of a wrongful act, such as a tort or breach of contract. Here there is no difficulty over title to sue: for obvious reasons, the proper plaintiff is the victim who could have sued for damages. If you profit from wrongfully using my car as a minicab, the obvious plaintiff is myself.

(3) Dealings with property

1-17   Thirdly, a right to restitution may arise from dealings with property derived from, or representing, something which someone else owns or has a claim to. The classic example is tracing, arising where assets representing my property come into your hands. Here again, there is little difficulty; that person has automatic title to sue. If, for instance, my trustee steals trust property, sells it for £1,000, and gives the £1,000 to you, I have a claim against the £1,000 in your hands[20].

1-18   The negative proposition is that where the source of the unjustified enrichment claim is a transfer of value by the plaintiff (e.g. a payment of money, or a service rendered), the latter does not have title to sue unless he intended to act at his own expense. In particular, if he looked to a

---

20   See below, Chapter 10.

third party for reimbursement, it is that third party who is the proper plaintiff. (Compare the example above, where you improve my land Blackacre under a contract with X). Why should this be? The reason, it is suggested, lies in the law of contract and in the distribution of risks normally associated with it. *Prima facie* a contractor takes the risk that his co-contractor will not prove creditworthy. If he wishes to obtain a guarantee of payment from somebody else, he should stipulate for it: if he does not, then there is no reason why, as regards him, any gain should not lie where it falls.

Multiple claimants

If the requirement of enrichment 'at the plaintiff's expense' is indeed merely an aspect of title to sue, it follows that there is no reason in principle why a given enrichment should not give rise to two or more claimants. Assume a trustee, appointed as such to a directorship of a company in which the trust owns shares, uses corporate information to make a secret profit for himself. As trustee he must on principle pay that profit to the trust: as director, to the company. Again, take the difficult case of *Reading v. Att-Gen*[21], where an Army sergeant on duty in Egypt took bribes to smuggle goods past Egyptian customs posts. The Crown successfully claimed to retain these in its capacity of employer: but there seems no reason why the Egyptian Government should not equally have maintained a claim on the basis that Reading had accepted payments rightfully due to them.

1-19

This, of course, gives rise to one obvious problem. There is nothing wrong as such with the trustee or Sergeant Reading being liable to two potential plaintiffs: on the other hand, what if they are actually sued by both? It does seem unfair that they should be liable twice over. This thorny question has hitherto not arisen in English law: but a possible answer to it is canvassed at para. 15-13 below.

3   UNJUSTIFIED ENRICHMENT AND OTHER FORMS OF LIABILITY

Since English law knows no unified 'action for unjustified enrichment' in the same sense as it has a general concept of an 'action in tort' or 'action on a contract'[22], there is no absolute distinction between unjustified enrichment and other forms of action. We have already

1-20

---

[21]   [1951] A.C. 507.

[22]   Indeed it does not even have a principle that monies paid but not owing are *prima facie* recoverable: see *Woolwich Building Society v. IRC (No. 2)* [1992] 3 All E.R. 737, 759 (Lord Goff).

mentioned in passing that resulting and constructive trusts on occasion remedy unjustified enrichment[23], even though that is not their only function. Similarly, the measure of damages in tort and contract may sometimes be aimed in practice at removing gain, rather than their official purpose of compensating loss. Thus in *Wrotham Park Estates v. Parkside Homes*[24] Brightman J fixed the measure of damages for breach of a restrictive covenant at the extra profit made by the defendant as a result of the breach: again, the possibility of punitive damages for torts aimed at making a profit[25], and the liability of a wrongful user of goods to pay a reasonable hire charge[26], are other cases in point.

Nevertheless, these are exceptional situations, and there are important differences of principle between restitution and other heads of liability, which it is worth briefly pointing out.

Tort

1-21 Restitution claims may, of course, duplicate other claims: thus the same facts may well allow alternative claims in tort and in unjustified enrichment. Suppose you deceive me into paying you £1,000. I can claim this sum from you in two ways: either in tort on the basis that I have lost it, or in unjustified enrichment on the basis that you have got it. It makes no difference which I choose (unless perhaps you are bankrupt, since then a constructive trust may come to my aid if I allege unjustified enrichment, but not in tort). There are nevertheless two essential differences between the two kinds of liability.

1-22 First, tort invariably depends on the defendant or someone connected with him having wrongfully done or omitted to do something (government compensation for criminal injuries compensates for injury, but does not count as tort). Unjustified enrichment does not. If a third party X steals my car, sells it and credits your bank account with the proceeds you must return them, however innocent you were[27]: the essence of the action is unjust enrichment, not wrong[28]. Indeed, there is no need for any human agency at all to give rise to a right to restitution; if a freak electrical storm were to cause a bank computer to transfer £1,000 capriciously from my account to yours, you would have to refund the money.

---

[23] E.g. in cases of mistake, under the rule in *Chase Manhattan Bank v. Israel-British Bank* [1979] 3 All E.R. 1025; para. 3–09 below.

[24] [1974] 2 All E.R. 321. But *cf Surrey CC v. Bredero Homes* [1993] 3 All E.R. 705.

[25] As in, e.g. *Broome v. Cassell* [1972] A.C. 1027.

[26] *Cf Strand Electric v. Brisford Entertainments* [1952] 2 Q.B. 246.

[27] Below, Chapter 10.

[28] *Cf Lipkin Gorman v. Karpnale* [1992] 4 All E.R. 512, 527 (Lord Goff).

Of course, some unjust enrichment liability does depend on a wrongful act. One cannot, for instance, bring waiver of tort unless there was a tort to waive in the first place. But the connection here is entirely contingent, and does not alter the general point.

Secondly, the measure of recovery is different: in tort it is loss, in unjustified enrichment, gain. Suppose you steal my car, worth £10,000. If you sell it for £12,000 I will be well advised to sue for your enrichment: on the other hand, if you only sell it for its actual value and I can prove consequential loss, I will do better in tort. Of course, this difference can be fudged. In the example of money obtained by deceit, it does not matter because loss precisely equals gain. Again, the computation of loss in tort is problematical, and at times the best approximation may be the defendant's gain (e.g. in an action for wrongfully using my goods, the hire charge I might reasonably have asked for may be the best way of computing my loss).

1-23

Contract[29]

Contract, like tort, can duplicate unjustified enrichment. If I pay you £5,000 for a car and you wrongfully fail to deliver it, then (assuming the car was actually worth £5,000) it does not matter whether I sue for breach of contract or money paid for a consideration that totally fails: I recover £5,000. Again, assume I contract to build you a house: the contract provides that if you wrongfully put an end to it, for instance by turning me off the site without good reason, then you are to pay me the reasonable value of any work done. If you do turn me out, it does not matter whether I base my claim for the value of the work done on the terms of the contract or on the principles of *quantum meruit*: I still get it.

1-24

Nevertheless, in these cases the claims are not the same. Recovery in contract is measured quite differently from restitution, by the amount promised (or in case of breach by loss): gain, the hallmark of an unjustified enrichment claim, has nothing to do with it. If those sums happen to be the same, as they were in both the above examples, that is fortuitous. Thus, in the case of the car mentioned above, the equivalence depends on the car being worth exactly £5,000. If it had been worth £6,000 or £4,000, recovery for breach of contract would be adjusted accordingly, but recovery for failure of consideration would remain at the same figure: hence, in the latter but not the former case, it would have been worth suing in restitution and not in contract[30].

---

[29] For the full relationship between contract and restitution, see Chapter 6.

[30] E.g. *Wilkinson v. Lloyd* (1845) 7 Q.B. 27.

Property

1-25   In one sense all claims to vindicate property are unjustified enrichment claims. If you unlawfully refuse to give back my car, or to admit that you hold Blackacre on trust for me, you are unjustifiably enriched by the value of the car or Blackacre: you have something you ought not to have. But this is a trivial point, and there is no point in subsuming the whole of the law of property in this book as a result of it. Therefore claims to recover one's property, claims in conversion and their equitable equivalent, claims for knowing receipt of trust property, are not covered. It is best in the circumstances to limit the term 'unjustified enrichment' to claims to property arising other than from the fact that the item in question simply belongs to the plaintiff. Thus in order to bring a unjustified enrichment claim properly so called in respect of something in your hands, I normally have to show that my right to it arose from one of two features: *either* (a) from the fact of its having come into your hands, it not having belonged to me before: *or* (b) from the fact that it is derived from, or represents, other property which I own or have a claim to. An example of (a) is the beneficiary's claim in respect of profits made from trust property in a trustee's hands: it is only because the assets representing those profits came into the trustee's hands at all that the beneficiary has any right whatever to them. As for (b), the 'common law tracing' cases give the best instance: if you receive monies representing assets stolen from me, you come under a duty to refund, not because those monies belong to me, but because you received them[31].

A general principle of recovery?

1-26   *Dicta* on whether there is such a thing as a generalised right of restitution or recovery for unjustified enrichment are many, and frankly not very helpful. Lord Mansfield is well known for his espousal of the view that the action for money had and received, one of the mainstays of common law restitution, should generally apply where 'the defendant, upon the circumstances of the case, is obliged by the ties of natural justice and equity to refund the money'[32]. Scrutton LJ was less charitable in 1922, choosing to castigate the whole idea of generalised liability for unjustified enrichment as 'well-meaning sloppiness of thought'[33]. In 1943, by contrast, Lord Wright recognised that 'any civilised system of law is bound to provide remedies for cases of what has been called unjust

---

[31] See para. 10-02 ff below.

[32] *Moses v. Macferlan* (1760) 2 Burr. 1005, at p. 1012.

[33] *Holt v. Markham* [1923] 1 KB 504, 513. To be fair, the reference was strictly speaking to the common law action for money had and received.

enrichment or unjust benefit, that is to prevent a man from retaining the money of, or some benefit derived from, another which it is against conscience that he should keep'[34]. More recently, Lord Goff has been prepared to accept that there is a category of actions in restitution to which, generically, change of position is a defence[35]. It is possible to find *dicta*, more or less unguarded, in Australia[36] and Canada[37] recognising some sort of general right to recover unjust enrichment.

In fact, as anyone who thinks briefly might expect, the answer to the issue of whether there is a general right of recovery in English law for unjustified enrichment essentially depends on how one poses the question.   **1-27**

First, there is the obvious point already amply stressed above: if by a general principle we mean a rule that any enrichment falls to be reversed if it is somehow 'unfair' or 'inequitable', then there is no such thing in English law – nor, for that matter, in any other legal system.

There is a weaker version, such as appears in German law: any enrichment without specific justification[38] (for example gift, contract, obligation) *prima facie* falls to be neutralised. It is submitted that even this has its difficulties when applied to the English approach. You make a profit from breaking a contract with me, or you get paid £250 to beat me up. In neither case is it easy to see any legal justification for your profit: yet in neither case have I a claim in unjustified enrichment against you.

In fact, the approach of English law to unjustified enrichment is to treat the subject at a very low level of abstraction. Just as the law of tort, while subject to a number of common features (not normally very important ones[39]) is in practice regarded as a collection of discrete heads of liability, so with restitution. The individual heads of recovery – money paid by mistake, money paid under ineffective contracts, benefits freely accepted, and so on – are all largely subject to their own rules. True, a number of common threads run through them: concepts such as benefit, lack of donative intent, and bars to recovery such as officiousness, apply to virtually all of them. True also that, where appropriate, new heads of recovery for unjustified enrichment may be created[40]. Nevertheless, it remains true that (a) as a general rule, a given enrichment is shown to be   **1-28**

---

[34] *Fibrosa Spolka Akcyjna v. Fairbairn Lawson Combe Barbour Ltd.* [1943] A.C. 32, 61.

[35] *Lipkin Gorman v. Karpnale* [1992] 4 All E.R. 512, 532.

[36] E.g. *Pavey & Matthews v. Paul* (1987) 162 C.L.R. 227, 256; *ANZ v. Westpac* (1988) 164 CLR 662, 673.

[37] *Deglman v. Guaranty Trust* (1954) 3 D.L.R. 785, despite its age, is still most commonly cited. *Cf James More v. University of Ottawa* (1974) 49 D.L.R. (3d) 666, 676 ('The categories of restitution are never closed'); and see *Air Canada v. British Columbia* [1989] S.C.R. 1133, 1201, *per* La Forest J.

[38] 'ohne rechtlichen Grund' – German Civil Code, § 812.

[39] E.g. the principles of *volenti non fit injuria*.

[40] E.g. recovery of overpaid taxes: para. 13–05 below.

unjustified not by reference to an abstract principle but by analogy with existing heads of recovery[41]; and (b) a similar attitude is likely to be shown towards suggested new heads of recovery[42].

Why this attitude? The argument from certainty, together with English lawyers' innate dislike of abstraction, provide some explanation. Furthermore, there is also the experience of other areas of the law. General principles of contract and tort may exist: nevertheless, as a matter of practice, the most illuminating way of looking at both these has been as separate heads of liability or types of contract: attempts to generalise further have tended to be inaccurate or vacuous. So too, it is suggested, with unjustified enrichment.

---

[41] 'Although as yet there is in English law no general rule giving the plaintiff a right of recovery from a defendant who has been unjustly enriched at the plaintiff's expense, the concept of unjust enrichment lies at the heart of all the individual instances in which the law does give a right of recovery': Lord Browne-Wilkinson in *Woolwich Building Society v. Inland Revenue Comm'rs* [1992] 3 All E.R. 737, 780.

[42] 'As in so many other fields of English law, the occasions on which recovery is permitted have been built up on a case by case basis': Lord Browne-Wilkinson in *Woolwich Building Society v. Inland Revenue Com'rs* [1992] 3 All E.R. 737, 781.

CHAPTER 2

REMEDIES

1 INTRODUCTION

Oddly enough, a chapter on remedies in a book on restitution is much less necessary than a similar chapter in a book about a mainstream subject, such as (say) contract. Indeed, it is rather a misnomer, since there is no general category of remedies for unjust enrichment. Compare contract and tort; there, the law neatly divides into right and remedy, and having decided in the first stage of an action whether there is an (abstract) cause of action, it is not then difficult to list the possible responses to it (damages, debt, specific enforcement, etc.) and decide which to use[1]. But this is not the way we think about restitution. There is no such thing as an abstract 'cause of action in unjust enrichment'. On the contrary: when we talk about restitution, we mean those legal mechanisms that in fact serve to reverse unjust enrichment; for example, the action for money had and received, the constructive trust, rights of reverter, my right to claim assets in your hands on the basis that they represent property once owned by me, and so on. It is these institutions themselves that form the substantive law of restitution, and to this extent they comprise both right and remedy.

2 MEANS OF RECOVERY

Nevertheless, the legal mechanisms just referred to are worth a brief **2-02** coverage in their own right, even at this stage. They can generally be divided into four categories: (a) simple pecuniary liabilities; (b) constructive trusts and similar equitable doctrines; (c) tracing remedies, i.e. remedies against property representing, or derived from, something which the plaintiff owns or has an interest in; and (d) transfer of property by operation of law, including subrogation. This is not, of course, to say that the legal responses they represent are mutually exclusive. On the contrary, in many cases they overlap. To take one example, if I pay you £100 by mistake, both equity and common law intervene: I have the

---

[1]   For a neat example of the separation of right and remedy in contract, see *Moschi v. Lep Air Services* [1972] 2 All E.R. 393.

choice whether to invoke the law of money had and received or a constructive trust in order to get it back. Whichever I choose will depend on contingent factors, such as whether you are still solvent, or whether you still have the money.

Simple pecuniary liabilities

2-03   These correspond most closely to damages in the rest of the law of obligations and are, in a way, the natural way of dealing with unjust enrichment. Restitution, after all, exists to remedy events causing unjustified imbalances in wealth: and just as the obvious remedy for a tort is the award of a monetary sum approximating to the plaintiff's loss, so the obvious remedy for unjustified enrichment is the award of a payment representing the defendant's gain. Most gains, like most losses, can be plausibly turned into money.

In practice, the majority of unjustified enrichment claims do indeed give rise to a money claim. The reason is historical: most of the legal institutions which now are recognised as going to make up the law of unjustified enrichment started life as particular types of claim for a money sum.

Common law claims

2-04   At common law, the most important category of pecuniary recovery was (and is) the action for money had and received. In its simplest form this applies where the plaintiff's money finds its way into the defendant's hands, for instance, where the defendant has stolen it or received it from a thief (other than bona fide and for value[2]). Here it corresponds roughly to the action for conversion of goods, which does not lie in respect of money in the form of currency. But money had and received takes many other forms as well. It extends, for instance, to cases where a third party has paid money to the defendant to be passed on to the plaintiff, or the defendant has usurped the plaintiff's office (with its emoluments)[3] or received payment in fact due to the plaintiff[4]; to actions for waiver of tort, enabling the plaintiff to recover the profits made by the defendant from certain kinds of tortious behaviour[5]; and to the action for money paid by mistake, by compulsion or for a consideration that has totally failed[6].

---

2   See generally *Lipkin Gorman v. Karpnale* [1992] 4 All E.R. 512.
3   *Arris v. Stukeley* (1677) 2 Mod 260.
4   *Jacob v. Allen* (1703) Salk 27.
5   See para. 11-08 below.
6   See Chapters 3, 4, 6 and 7 below.

Secondly, there is the action for money paid at the plaintiff's request, available where you ask me to pay X £100 and I do so[7], or - by an extension of the concept of request - where I am forced (for example as a surety) to pay a debt properly chargeable to you[8].

2-05

Thirdly, there is the action for *quantum valebat* and *quantum meruit*, dealing with the case where I supply goods (*quantum valebat*) or services (*quantum meruit*) to you without a contract and which nevertheless you ought to have to pay for. At its simplest, this action forms the basis for liability based on free acceptance, as where you ask me to do something otherwise than as a favour and I do it. But it also extends to other situations, for instance where you render services by mistake, or under a proposed contract that fails to materialise[9].

2-06

Lastly at common law, it must not be forgotten that ordinary damages for tort or breach of contract occasionally serve a restitutionary purpose. If I use your car without your permission, for instance, there is some authority that my liability in damages for conversion can be reckoned not simply as your loss, but as the reasonable hire value of the car concerned - i.e. my profit, or the amount I have saved myself through using your car rather than hiring one of my own[10].

2-07

Common law restitutionary claims are treated as any other common law claim to money: the courts' power to provide pre-trial *Mareva* relief[11], and to give interest under s.35A of the Supreme Court Act 1981[12], apply to them as to any other.

Common law pecuniary claims and implied contract

The various common law heads of recovery used to be classified under the Romanistic heading 'quasi-contract'. In so far as this reflected the fact that they had to be classified somewhere, and that recovery was allowed as though the defendant had promised to make a payment, even though he had not, it did no harm: indeed, on occasion it did good, as where it took a given claim out of the law of tort for the purposes of the rule *actio personalis moritur cum persona*, or the old rule of bankruptcy law that tort claims were not provable[13]. On the other hand, use of contract

2-08

---

[7]   See para. 5-04 ff, below.

[8]   See para. 9-01 ff, below.

[9]   See para. 5-02 ff, below.

[10]   See para. 11-07, below.

[11]   I.e. to prevent the defendant disposing of his property so as to defeat a possible claim. E.g. Snell's, *Equity*, 29th ed., p.670.

[12]   See *B.P. (Exploration) v. Hunt* [1982] 1 All E.R. 925.

[13]   Abolished by the Law Reform (Miscellaneous Provisions) Act 1934 and the Insolvency Act 1985 respectively.

terminology gave rise to confusion elsewhere. In *Sinclair v. Brougham*[14], plaintiffs who lent money to a company in an *ultra vires* transaction were very nearly deprived of any remedy whatever on the basis that the company was congenitally incapable of promising to return an *ultra vires* loan and hence no action in quasi-contract could lie. They only succeeded because the House of Lords managed to find a proprietary remedy outside the field of quasi-contract to help them. Similarly, in *Morgan v. Ashcroft*[15] it was somehow thought relevant to a claim by a bookmaker for overpaid winnings that statute prohibited any action on a contract for sums wagered. Such reasoning to-day is, however, discredited and in the rest of this book the supposed connection between the common law restitutionary actions and the law of contract will, as far as possible, be ignored.

Other pecuniary claims

2-09   Not all simple pecuniary claims in restitution arise at common law. Equity is also a player in this market; just as it on occasion awards *in personam* compensation equivalent to damages[16], it sometimes awards a restitutionary cash sum. The action for profits made out of his position by a fiduciary, such as an agent[17], is one example: it creates a kind of 'equitable debt'. Indeed, there is no reason why a trustee who profits from making use of trust property should not be liable to a similar remedy (though in practice most beneficiary claimants will claim a constructive trust). Again, in *Ministry of Health v. Simpson*[18] it was held that underpaid beneficiaries or creditors of an estate had an *in personam* right of recovery against anyone overpaid out of the same estate; and to give yet a further example, a trustee can in certain cases sue the beneficiaries for reimbursement in respect of necessary services rendered to the trust estate[19]. Except for the *in personam* right under *Ministry of Health v. Simpson*, equitable claims of this sort carry interest under the court's inherent jurisdiction: in suitable cases this may include compound interest[20].

Yet other money claims are *sui generis*. The personal action available to a maritime salvor[21] is a case in point.

---

14 [1914] A.C. 398.
15 [1938] 2 K.B. 49.
16 E.g. compensation for breach of trust where no trust property remains in the defendant's hands.
17 *Boston Deep Sea Fishing v. Ansell* (1888) 39 Ch. D. 339.
18 [1951] A.C. 251.
19 *Hardoon v. Belilios* [1901] A.C. 118; para. 8-07 below.
20 See *Wallersteiner v. Moir (No. 2)* [1975] 1 All E.R. 849.
21 See para. 8-13 ff below.

Constructive trusts and similar cases

It is trite law that the constructive trust is not, as such, a remedy for   **2-10**
unjustified enrichment. It is more a general equitable device to remedy
certain defects in the rest of the law of obligations: witness its function in
enforcing agreements that would otherwise go unenforced (for example,
secret trusts, or conveyances subject to an obligation for the benefit of a
third party[22]), or in compensating for loss in cases of misdealing for
which the common law provides no remedy (e.g. the liability for
knowing assistance in a fraudulent breach of trust[23]).

Nevertheless, in practice the constructive trust often is pressed into
service to deal with straightforward unjustified enrichment, in particular
where the enrichment concerned survives in the hands of the defendant.
The best known example is the right of a beneficiary to lay claim to
profits made by a fiduciary from using trust property: if my trustee makes
a profit by using trust shares[24] or information coming to him as such[25],
then that profit is regarded as being held on trust for me. Other similar
instances include the mistaken payer's right to money in the hands of the
payee[26], and a contractor's rights to property transferred under a contract
later avoided on some equitable ground such as undue influence[27].

The advantages and disadvantages from the plaintiff's point of view   **2-11**
of the constructive trust in such situations are dealt with below. Most
importantly, it prevails in the event of bankruptcy, and also provides
further recovery if the defendant makes further profits out of the
property concerned.

In certain cases equity's intervention in respect of unjust enrichment
takes the form not of a constructive trust but of an equitable lien. One
example is the right given to an innocent improver of land to claim an
interest in land where he has spent money on it or otherwise enhanced
it with the express or tacit encouragement of the true owner[28].
Another may be the right of an underwriter to be subrogated to rights
of action otherwise vested in his assured, though the matter here is far
from certain[29].

---

[22] *Binions v. Evans* [1972] Ch. 359 is perhaps the best-known example of this process.

[23] Snell's *Equity*, 29th ed., p.193 ff. But *quaere* if this is a case of trust at all: see Professor Birks in McKendrick, *Commercial Aspects of Trusts and Fiduciary Obligations*, Ch. 8.

[24] *Re Macadam* [1946] Ch. 73.

[25] As happened in *Phipps v. Boardman* [1967] 2 A.C. 46: see Wilberforce J's original order at [1964] 2 All E.R. 187, 208.

[26] *Chase Manhattan Bank v. Israel-British Bank* [1979] 3 All E.R. 1025.

[27] Hence cases such as *Bank of Credit & Commerce International v. Aboody* [1990] 1 Q.B. 923.

[28] *Unity Joint Stock Bank v. King* (1858) 25 Beav 72; Ch. III, below.

[29] The nature of the underwriter's interest was left open in *Lord Napier & Ettrick v. Hunter* [1993] 1 All E.R.385.

Legal title: restitution and property

2-12   Constructive trusts and equitable liens vest a more or less extensive equitable title in someone who would not otherwise have it. On occasion, however, the law deals with unjust enrichment in a slightly cruder way, by manipulating legal title itself.

Assume, for example, that you deceive me into making a gift to you of my car. Alternatively, assume you buy my car, but the underlying contract of sale was induced by fraud[30]. In either case, I can avoid the transaction: gifts and contracts induced by fraud are voidable. But you, of course, still have the car. The way in which the law deals with this unjustified enrichment on your part is by causing legal title in it to re-vest in me by operation of law[31]. Once this has happened I am treated as owner for all purposes: for instance, if you sell the car to an innocent third party while still in possession of it, then unless he can bring himself within one of the exceptions to *nemo dat*[32], he gets no title to it[33].

Tracing[34]

2-13   Tracing is not strictly a remedy at all, rather a bolt-on extension of the law of property which acts as an adjunct to other restitutionary institutions, such as constructive trusts and claims for money had and received. Its distinctive feature arises as follows. Most claims to restitution are concerned (a) with the actual money or assets whose arrival in the defendant's hands is alleged to represent an unjustified enrichment on the latter's part under one of the established heads of restitutionary recovery; and (b) with the liability of the original recipient of the benefit, and no-one else. But the claimant may want to go further than this. Property that went to enrich X unjustly may have found its way into Y's hands, and the claimant may want to recover it from Y; again, X may have sold or given away what he actually received, but still be in possession of some thing or fund; in which case the claimant may be interested in laying claim to that. It is claims of this sort that fall to be dealt with by tracing.

For example, suppose you deceive me into giving you my car, or I pay you £100 by mistake, or you (being my agent) receive a bribe from a third party. There is no doubt that I can get the car, the £100 or the bribe from you: these all represent well-established and uncontroversial

---

[30] In practice the fraud normally consists of paying for the vehicle with a worthless cheque.

[31] E.g. *Car & Universal Finance v. Caldwell* [1965] 1 Q.B. 525.

[32] Most plausibly, s. 9 of the Factors Act 1889: *Newtons of Wembley v. Williams* [1965] 1 Q.B. 560.

[33] *Car & Universal v. Caldwell*, above.

[34] See Chapter 10 below, on Restitution through Third Parties.

heads of unjust enrichment. But what if you exchange the car for a van, or give the £100 or the bribe to charity? Tracing principles decide whether I have any rights against the van in your hands, or the money in the charity's.

One further distinction is worth noting at this stage. In so far as tracing is used to give the plaintiff a common law claim, such as money had and received, or a claim to legal ownership of a chattel, it is known as 'common law tracing': 'equitable tracing' covers the situation where the plaintiff seeks to enforce an equitable right, such as a declaration that certain assets are held on trust for him, or an *in personam* claim such as arose in *Ministry of Health v. Simpson*[35]. **2-14**

Indeed, sometimes the same facts can give rise to both types of claim. If an agent steals his principal's cheque, cashes it and buys a car with the proceeds, the principal can claim the car either by a common law tracing claim (relying on his erstwhile legal ownership of the cheque) or in equity (founding on the fact that his agent was in a fiduciary position as against him).

Why bother about the distinction between the two sorts of tracing? The answer is twofold. First there is the difference in outcome: a legal tracing claim cannot give rise to an equitable right, or *vice versa*. And secondly, the substantive rules about what assets in the defendant's hands the plaintiff can identify with his original loss and thus appropriate to his claim differ according to which variety of tracing are in issue; a matter dealt with in greater detail in Chapter 10, below.

Subrogation[36]

Subrogation involves the transfer by operation of law of the benefit of some right from A to B. Its relevance to restitution is that, as often as not, this transfer takes place in order to reverse what would otherwise be unjust enrichment. The enrichment may be that either of A himself, or alternatively of X, the person subject to the obligation, who would otherwise escape its effect (or his general creditors). An example of the first type of subrogation is the underwriter's right to take over claims vested in the assured, who could otherwise recover twice[37]: of the second, the ability of a surety to enforce for his own benefit securities given by the principal debtor, whose creditors would otherwise get an undeserved windfall[38]. **2-15**

---

[35] [1951] A.C. 251.
[36] Chapter 12 below.
[37] Below, para. 12-09.
[38] Below, para. 12-08.

In its second manifestation subrogation acts to some extent as a mirror image of tracing: tracing transfers the plaintiff's claim to a positive asset of the defendant, subrogation to a negative one. Two examples clarify the point. Suppose my trustee steals £1,000 from the trust fund and gives it to you, you receiving it in bad faith. If you use the £1,000 to buy a picture, I can claim the picture[39]: if, by contrast, you used it to pay off the mortgage on your house, I can equally claim to take over the rights of the mortgagee[40]. Again, assume I lend you money which, for some reason, turns out irrecoverable: but you use that money to pay off lawful debts of yours. I can prevent you being unjustifiably enriched by being subrogated to your creditors' rights[41].

3 RESTITUTION: CHOICE OF REMEDIES

2-16   As in other areas of the law, it is open to a restitution claimant to choose the cause of action most advantageous to him: and, again as elsewhere, this is often an significant right. It is by no means rare for a given instance of unjustified enrichment to give rise to more than one possible restitutionary response.

Assume, for the sake of argument, that I pay you £1,000 by mistake. I can make a personal claim for £1,000 from you as money had and received to your use. Further and alternatively, if you still have the £1,000 in your bank, I can claim a constructive trust over that part of your balance. If you do not still have the original money, but you do have gilt-edged stock that you bought using it, I can claim the stock (or at least a proportionate interest in it). And if you used it to pay off your mortgage, I may (as pointed out in the preceding paragraph) have a claim to be your secured creditor to the amount of £1,000.

2-17   I have a complete choice between which of these rights I choose to exercise. Nevertheless, there are substantial differences between them: in particular, between pecuniary remedies and the others. Pecuniary remedies, for instance, have the advantage of providing the plaintiff with the full amount of the defendant's gain, whatever the latter did with it, and whatever may have happened since then (assuming, for the moment, that the defence of change of position does not apply[42]). On the other hand, they have the disadvantage of abating in insolvency. Proprietary claims, by contrast, have their own advantages and drawbacks. If

---

[39] Under the principle in e.g. *Pennell v. Deffell* (1853) 4 De G M & G 372.

[40] By analogy to e.g. *Thurstan v. Nottingham Permanent Building Society* [1903] A.C. 6.

[41] *Thurstan's* case, above.

[42] On change of position, see para. 15-09 below.

established, they protect a plaintiff against an insolvent defendant[43]: furthermore, they may provide a useful windfall in the case of rising values. If I pay you £1,000 by mistake and you buy shares with it that are now worth £2,000, a personal claim would yield £1,000 plus interest, whereas a proprietary one would provide £2,000. Again, proprietary claims engender a right in the claimant to obtain an injunction *pendente lite* to protect assets subject to them[44]. Admittedly, this advantage is much less significant since the rise of the *Mareva* jurisdiction[45] to give some protection in respect of personal claims. Nevertheless, it may still be important and tactically relevant. Thus a *Mareva* injunction will not protect a plaintiff against an insolvent's general creditors[46], but an injunction to protect property in dispute will: again, the latter type of injunction is open to the County Court, whereas a *Mareva* injunction is not. On the other hand, to assert a constructive trust or equitable lien, the restitution plaintiff may have a more difficult task. Not only does he face the task of showing that a particular piece of his property represents his claim; he is, in any event, limited to such of the value of that property as the defendant still has at the time of the action. One cannot assert an equitable interest over something that is not there.

---

[43] Subject to possible claims for the general expenses of his insolvency: *cf* e.g. *Re Berkeley Applegate [No. 2]* (1988) 3 All E.R. 71.

[44] R.S.C., Ord.29, r.2.

[45] I.e. the courts' jurisdiction to limit a defendant's disposal of his assets where that would subvert even a mere personal claim.

[46] *The Angel Bell* [1980] 1 All E.R. 480; *Bekhor v. Bilton* [1981] 2 All E.R. 564, 577.

CHAPTER 3

MISTAKE

1 INTRODUCTION

Restitution of benefits rendered by mistake is an obvious head of recovery in respect of unjustified enrichment. If I claim to be allowed to retain a benefit which you only provided to me because at the time you were labouring under some mistake, this requires, at the very least, some justification.

3-01

Having said this, however, a number of preliminary points fall to be made before going on to deal with the details of recovery.

3-02

To begin with, although the basis of relief for mistake is that mistaken assent deserves less weight than real assent, the boundary between the two is hazy rather than clear-cut: one cannot divide benefit-conferring acts neatly or infallibly into 'voluntary' and 'mistaken'. It is perfectly possible for a person to benefit another under the influence of given false belief, and yet for his act to be 'voluntary' in any normal meaning of the term. Suppose I give you £5,000 worth of shares as a reward for having passed the Bar examination. If, unknown to me, you had in fact failed, I can argue convincingly that I did not act voluntarily and you ought in the circumstances to give back the shares (or perhaps account for their value) to me. But change the facts slightly: you did pass the examination, but when I gave you the shares I remained in ignorance of some financial development in markets abroad that was bound to lead to their doubling in value in a few days. In such circumstances there is no doubt that I acted under a misapprehension: nevertheless, it is submitted that most people would say I acted voluntarily.

Secondly, one has to be careful to circumscribe restitution for mistake. Even where clearly mistaken, there are a number of cases where a person fairly obviously ought to be denied recovery. For instance, it must be open to me, when rendering a benefit to you, expressly or implicitly to accept the risk that I may be mistaken on a given point. Again, I may choose to compromise a claim you bring against me: assuming I do so on a basis of inadequate information, and the claim was not in fact a good one after all, nevertheless the value of upholding compromises will have to be set against what would otherwise be a clear right of recovery. These matters are dealt with more fully below.

3-03

3–04   Thirdly, the law of contract impinges heavily on this part of the law, in particular where the money it is sought to recover, (or for that matter any other benefit) was paid under a contract which itself is later successfully impugned for mistake. Because this raises a number of specific issues connected with the law of contract, this chapter will not cover payments made in accordance with an apparently valid contract. Contractual restitution cases of this sort are dealt with elsewhere[1].

3–05   Fourthly, here as in a number of other areas of restitution, the rules of recovery depend on the sort of benefit conferred: payment of money, rendering of services, and so on. This is partly a matter of history – money paid by mistake being recovered by the action for money had and received, improvements to land through the law of trusts, for instance. But quite independently of this factor, there is (as we shall see) good reason for some of these distinctions.

2   THE DEFINITION OF 'MISTAKE'

3–06   'Mistake' is a protean term. For the purpose of most of this chapter, it will be taken to mean any mistake as to a matter of present fact. Though this may in suitable cases include beliefs as to others' opinion, or as to intention[2], it does not include mistake as to future events. This is not to say that mistakes as to the future cannot ground restitution. On the contrary, they clearly can; witness the actions for money paid for a consideration that has totally failed, or services rendered in the expectation of future contractual relations that never eventualise. Nevertheless, the law of restitution is (rightly) slower to compensate for disappointed hopes than for blighted intentions; hence the principles that apply are rather different, and fall to be dealt with elsewhere[3].

As for mistake of law, this is a difficult area, and there are signs that it may be being gradually assimilated to mistake of fact. Nevertheless, at present it remains a subject treated very differently and for that reason deserves a section to itself. This appears at the end of the chapter.

---

[1]   See Chapter 6 below.

[2]   As in the law of contract: "the state of a man's mind is as much a fact as the state of his digestion", *per* Bowen LJ in *Edgington v. Fitzmaurice* (1885) 29 Ch. D. 459.

[3]   Especially in Chapters 5 and 6.

3 MONEY PAID BY MISTAKE

The principle of recovery

Money paid by mistake of fact is *prima facie* recoverable from the payee as money had and received[4]. It does not matter whether the recipient knew of the mistake[5], nor what the nature of the payment was. As appears below, gifts of money (as in the examination example above) are recoverable in the same way as payments supposedly made under a contract (as where I inadvertently pay your bill twice).

3-07

As mentioned above, the limitation to mistake of fact is deliberate: mistake of law may equally precipitate recovery, but the rules are sufficiently different to justify separate treatment.

The mistake

Grant that money paid by mistake is recoverable: what mistakes count for these purposes? There is no doubt that the net is drawn wide. It includes mistakes due to the payer's own fault[6], and rightly so: there is no reason why one man's negligence should be another man's windfall. Furthermore, recovery goes beyond cases where the payer believed himself legally obliged to pay[7]. Thus a gift may be recovered[8], as may a payment inadvertently made by a bank on a countermanded cheque[9], even though in neither case was there a question of the payer being under any obligation whatever to the payee[10].

3-08

It has been argued, with engaging simplicity[11], that there should on principle be no limitations at all on operative mistakes, and that the claimant should merely have to show that he was mistaken and that this

---

[4] See *Kelly v. Solari* (1841) 9 M & W 54: *Norwich Union Fire Insurance v. Price* [1934] A.C. 670: *Rover International v. Cannon Film Sales* [1989] 3 All E.R. 423.

[5] The insured in *Norwich Union Fire Insurance v. Price*, note above, and *Jones v. Waring & Gillow* [1926] A.C. 696, acted entirely innocently.

[6] *Kelly v. Solari* (1841) 9 M & W 54, 59; *Rover International v. Cannon Film Sales* [1989] 3 All E.R. 423, 431.

[7] Unless statute impliedly or expressly applies otherwise. This best explains *Morgan v. Ashcroft* [1938] 1 K.B. 49.

[8] E.g. *Larner v. L.C.C.* [1949] 2 K.B. 683 (*ex gratia* payment).

[9] *Barclays Bank v. W.J. Simms* [1979] 3 All E.R. 522. Earlier authorities apparently requiring a mistake as to obligation must now be read in the light of this decision.

[10] In the case of the cheque, see Bills of Exchange Act 1882, s. 53(1).

[11] And some support by Goff J. in *Barclays Bank v. W.J. Simms* [1979] 3 All E.R. 522: see pp.532-535, *passim*.

in fact caused him to pay. Any necessary protection for the payee, it is argued, should come from the defence of change of position; however small the mistake, a volunteer[12] who has not relied on the gift deserves no indulgence at all. But this must be doubtful[13], if only because of the argument outlined above, that a payment may be 'voluntary' despite being the result of a mistake of fact. Assume I give £1,000 to my niece as a birthday present, not realising that she has just married a man I violently dislike, or for that matter that the value of my share portfolio has fallen substantially within the last hour. It is suggested that any attempt by me to recover the £1,000, on the basis that had I been properly informed I should have repented of my generosity, would fail: my gift, albeit mistaken, was the result of my own free will[14].

If this is so, we need a criterion to distinguish those payments that should be regarded as voluntary and hence irrecoverable. In the absence of evidence of the parties' intent, it is suggested that the best criterion is that of the reasonable bystander. If such a person, knowing the facts behind the payment but not the individual characteristics of the parties, would have regarded the mistake as immaterial, then the money will be irrecoverable: otherwise it can *prima facie* be recovered back.

Money paid by mistake: a further means of recovery

3-09   We have seen that money paid by mistake is recoverable at common law as money had and received. But this is not the only remedy. In *Chase Manhattan NV v. Israel-British Bank*[15], it was held that an alternative means of recovery was available by way of constructive trust. Hence where the plaintiffs inadvertently credited $1 million twice to a payee who subsequently became insolvent, they were able to claim the second payment from the liquidator (who still held it), on the basis that it was held on constructive trust for them. The reasoning behind this is not entirely clear, but the best justification for it is that, whatever their opinion with regard to legal title in the second payment, the plaintiffs

---

12   Though not a contractor receiving money in accordance with the contract. The payer would first have to get rid of the contract; and, as appears below, a contract is more difficult to impugn for mistake than a mere gift.

13   Compare Lord Wright in *Norwich Union Fire Insurance v. Price* [1934] A.C. 455, 463: "It is, however, essential that the mistake relied on should be of such a nature that it can properly be described as a mistake in respect of the underlying assumption of the contract or transaction or as being fundamental or basic." The point was left open in the Australian case of *ANZ v. Westpac* (1988) 164 C.L.R. 662, 671–672.

14   It will not do here to say that I intended to pay 'in any event'. On the contrary, I did not; to say I should be treated as though I had done so is of course possible, but merely begs the question.

15   [1979] 3 All E.R. 1025.

never intended to confer any equitable ownership on the defendants[16]. (But if so, it seems arguable that the trust ought to have been regarded as resulting rather than constructive[17]).

4 PROPERTY TRANSFERRED BY MISTAKE

One might have thought property transferred by mistake should be on the same footing as money paid: if my error in paying you £100 *prima facie* makes it unjustifiable for you to keep the money, why should not my error in giving you a cow (or a house) equally put you under a duty to make restitution?   **3-10**

A moment's thought, however, shows that there is a vital difference. Money is a fungible: it, or its equivalent, can always be returned. Not so, however, with anything else. It is true that, if you still have the cow (or the house), you can give it back *in specie*: but if you do not, making you recompense me for it involves a forced exchange (i.e. you are forced to pay for something you may not have wanted at all, or been prepared to pay for in full even if you did[18]). For this reason, the law does not start from the '*prima facie* recoverable' position applicable to money payments. Instead, it deals with the question piecemeal, depending on the background to the transaction and the nature of the mistake and the remedy sought.

Transfers between contracting parties

These are dealt with elsewhere: see above.   **3-11**

Gifts

The gift of a chattel is, it would seem, entirely void if made under a fundamental mistake, for instance, as to who the donee is. Suppose you live in the same house as a friend of mine and telephone me in his name asking me to give you my old car; I leave it outside your gate, and you take it. It is suggested that legal title would remain in me; I never intended to give anything to you at all, and I could recover the car from you or any subsequent transferee – however innocent – simply by suing in conversion[19].   **3-12**

---

[16] *Cf* Millett J. in *Eldan Services v. Chandag Motors* [1990] 3 All E.R. 459, 461-462. Hence the remedy did not apply to what was effectively a claim for failure of consideration.

[17] See Chapter 7, below.

[18] See Chapter 14, below.

[19] This would seem to be *a fortiori* to the facts in *Cundy v. Lindsay* (1878) 3 App. Cas. 459.

Gifts of other property, where writing of some sort is required to transfer legal title, are treated slightly differently. Where the question is one of fundamental mistake, a transfer in writing may be impeached by invoking the doctrine of *non est factum*, which applies where the transferor was fundamentally mistaken as to the effect of his action. But this is subject to severe limitations. First, *non est factum* is limited to drastic mistakes; errors not going to the fundamental nature of the transaction do not count[20]. Secondly, it is negatived by negligence on the part of the transferor[21], at least as against an innocent transferee for value[22].

3-13   What of less fundamental mistakes? If a gift is obtained by misrepresentation on the part of the donee, it seems (by analogy with the law of contract) that it is voidable, and the donor can take steps to annul it[23]. In the case of a chattel, such steps presumably cause legal title to re-vest in the donor (unless the rights of a *bona fide* purchaser have intervened meanwhile[24]). In the case of other property, a trust will no doubt be raised in favour of the donor[25].

Absent misrepresentation, and assuming that the mistake is not fundamental enough to prevent property passing, there are problems about allowing a common law claim for the value of the thing transferred, since effectively it would allow a donor unilaterally to turn a mistaken gift into a sale and offend the principle against forced exchange. Nevertheless, such a claim could conceivably succeed on the analogy of *quantum valebat*. True, *quantum valebat* is normally limited to goods accepted in circumstances suggesting an intention to charge, which *ex hypothesi* a gift is not: but arguably, mistake on the part of the donor may be sufficient to overcome any argument based on gratuitous intent. The moral case for the donor is undeniable: furthermore, the recent acceptance of a general defence of change of position[26] suggests that adequate protection can be given to the donee who may have passed the gift on or sold it and frittered away the proceeds.

In any case the presence or absence of a common law remedy may not be very important in practice. There is a series of cases to the effect that gifts by deed can be revoked in equity if made under a mistake[27];

---

20 *Saunders v. Anglia Building Society* [1971] A.C. 1004.

21 *Ibid.*

22 *UDT v. Western* (1976) Q.B. 513.

23 *Re Glubb* [1900] 1 Ch. 354 .

24 Again, by analogy with property transferred under a contract later annulled for misrepresentation: *Car & Universal Finance v. Caldwell* [1965] 1 Q.B. 525.

25 *Cf* the analogous position where a transfer valid at common law is avoided by the provisions of the Insolvency Act 1986: e.g. *Re French's Wine Bar* [1987] B.C.L.C. 499.

26 On which generally see Chapter 15 below.

27 *Hood of Avalon (Lady) v. McKinnon* [1909] 1 Ch. 476; *Ellis v. Ellis* [1909] 26 T.L.R. 166.

and there seems no reason not to extend the same principle to any form of property, such as things in action, that does not pass by mere delivery. Similarly, when Goulding J decided in *Chase Manhattan NV v. Israel-British Bank*[28] that mistaken payments were held on constructive trust, he clearly thought that property mistakenly transferred stood on the same footing[29]. If this is right, then whatever the position at law, a mistaken gift is presumably held on constructive trust for the donor to the extent that the donee still has it or its proceeds.

Other non-contractual transfers

Assume I transfer something to you thinking I am bound to do so by contract (whether the contract was with you yourself or with a third party). I later discover that the contract did not in fact require me to make the transfer concerned. For example, I agree to sell you a quantity of goods but mistakenly over-deliver: or, having built you a house, I leave materials on site that (I wrongly think) the contract requires me to hand over to you. Here there is almost certainly an intention to pass property, so no claim can be made on the basis of retained ownership: so the question is whether I can claim either the value of what I have transferred, or perhaps some equitable relief.   **3-14**

We begin with value claims. In sales of goods, the matter of over-delivery is dealt with by statute. Assuming the buyer accepts the increased quantity (which he need not), he must pay for the excess[30]). Moreover (and this is a slightly peculiar feature of a restitutionary claim), he must pay at the contract rate, not simply the value of the excess goods[31].

Elsewhere, as in the case of the building contract, or for that matter a sale of goods where I deliver extra goods which happen to be of a different sort from those contracted for[32], the statute does not apply. Here, it is suggested that I can *prima facie* recover a reasonable price for the overplus (assuming you do not take steps to reject it). However, this is arguably on the basis, not so much of mistake, as the wider principle that a restitutionary claim lies for goods or services freely accepted where payment was clearly expected for them[33]. True, if you shared my mistake   **3-15**

---

28 [1979] 3 All E.R. 1025

29 See [1979] 3 All E.R. 1025, 1031, where he cited *Scott on Trusts*, 3rd ed., Vol. 5, p.3428, to that effect.

30 Sale of Goods Act 1979, s. 30(1).

31 Sale of Goods Act 1979, s. 30(4).

32 Section 30(4) explicitly allows the buyer to reject the non-conforming goods, but does not say what happens if he accepts them.

33 Chapter 5 below.

about the meaning of the contract, you might argue that there was no genuine free acceptance: on principle, acceptance due to error often ought not to count as free[34]. But it is submitted that such a plea is unlikely to attract much sympathy here. You have indisputably had the benefit of the property (and if you have not, for instance because you have lost it or given it away, you may well be able to shelter behind a defence of change of position[35]); furthermore, you could presumably have sought advice on the terms of the contract before accepting the goods.

3-16 So much for value claims. What about equitable claims based on a constructive trust? If I agree to sell you 10 loads of cement but instead deliver 11 can I claim a constructive trust over the eleventh – if, of course, you still have it and I can identify it[36]? Or, if I agree to sell you part of Blackacre and then mistakenly convey the whole of it, can I claim a trust of the excess? The answer in both cases seems to be yes: in the case of land by direct authority[37], elsewhere by the analogy of *Chase Manhattan v. Israel-British Bank*[38], above.

5 SERVICES RENDERED BY MISTAKE

Services rendered under contracts ineffective for mistake

3-17 This is dealt with elsewhere: see Chapter 6.

Other services rendered under a mistake

The prima facie rule: no recovery

3-18 Unlike money and (to a lesser extent) property, the law starts from a prejudice against restitutionary recovery for services rendered by mistake. This is for a number of reasons. One is largely psychological. Money can very often be repaid, and property returned *in specie*. If this happens, things *look* very tidy: no–one (at least in theory) is any worse off. Services, by contrast, are untidy: they cannot be given back as such.

---

[34] See para. 5-06 ff below.

[35] Below, Chapter 15.

[36] Does it matter that in practice it is likely to be impossible to identify which particular bag represented the excess? Presumably not.

[37] *Harris v. Pepperell* (1867) L.R. 5 Eq 1: *cf* the Canadian case of *Eadie v. Township of Brantford* (1967) 63 D.L.R. (2d) 561.

[38] [1979] 3 All E.R. 1025.

Secondly, there is the obvious point that while money never, and property sometimes, raises the problem of forced exchange, restitution for services always does. If I do something for you by mistake, the only way to recompense me is effectively to force you to buy something from me which you never agreed to pay me for in the first place.

Thirdly, while it is true that services can be requested or accepted in advance, it is normally unreal to talk about them being accepted or rejected after the event. Without your knowledge I credit your account with £1,000 or leave a case of wine on your doorstep; you can either accept or decline the credit, accept the wine or tell me you do not want it[39]. But if I do something for you, such as cleaning your car, that is it. If you did not ask me to do it[40], there is nothing that can be done about it now[41]; if you did ask me, I can recover for services rendered at your request.

Hence the general assumption that a person rendering services (rather than paying money or transferring goods) is generally deemed to do so at his own risk, even as regards mistake. It is the view epitomised, for instance, by *Falcke v. Scottish Imperial Assurance Co.*[42]. The plaintiff paid premiums to keep alive an insurance policy which he wrongly thought that he had an interest. When he found he had not, he failed to obtain any sort of relief against the true owner.

The exceptions to the rule against restitution

Acceptance

Exceptionally, some services – or rather the benefit of them – can be meaningfully accepted or rejected *ex post facto*. Here acceptance can give rise to a duty to pay. If you owe X £1,000 and I pay X off in your name but without your authority, you can choose whether to ratify the payment and take the discharge. If you do, then I can claim £1,000[43]

3-19

---

[39] *Cf Re Paradise Motor Co.* [1968] 2 All E.R. 625; even if property has passed in a purported gift, it may still be disclaimed.

[40] Or acquiesce in my doing so.

[41] *Cf* Pollock CB's often-quoted canard in *Taylor v. Laird* (1856) 25 L.J. Ex. 329, 332: "One cleans another's shoes; what can the other do but put them on?"

[42] (1886) 34 Ch. D. 234. It is true that the case is hardly strong authority. The plaintiff failed to establish his mistake on the facts: the defendant had no chance to reject the benefit: and the plaintiff was claiming, not recompense, but a lien on the policy. But there are still strong *dicta* against recovery even as a matter of principle.

[43] But what happens if you could have settled with X by paying him £900? Does this sum represent the amount of your benefit, and hence limit my recovery: or are you, by your acceptance, precluded from denying that you have benefited by £1,000?

from you as a benefit freely accepted. If you do not, the debt remains undischarged and there is, as such, no benefit to pay for[44]. Of course this only applies where you do have the choice. If, as on the facts of *Boulton v. Jones*[45], you yourself act under a mistake in accepting the benefit, you have not (it is submitted) really accepted it at all, and hence no claim lies against you[46]. Again, assume you buy a house subject to a mortgage to a bank, and I, thinking the house is mine, discharge the mortgage. The house is *ipso facto* released, whether you like it or not: for this reason I have no claim against you[47].

Acquiescence

3-20   This is a sort of half-way house between free acceptance and outight refusal. If you watch me doing something for you and say nothing, the equity against you becomes stronger than if you did not know what was happening: it is nevertheless still a good deal weaker than if you asked me to do it, or took positive steps to appropriate the benefit of what I had done. Nevertheless, acquiescence seems, in general, to be equiparated to acceptance[48].

Most of the cases here concern improvements to land (though there is no reason why the principle should not apply to chattels as well[49]). Thus in *Unity Joint Stock Banking Co. v. King*[50] a farmer's two sons, thinking they owned certain land which in fact belonged to their father, improved a piece of it to the extent of some £200 by building granaries on it. The farmer stood by and let them. The sons were held entitled as against him to a lien for their improvements. Again, in *Lee-Parker v. Izzett (No. 2)*[51] the claimant, as a result of a confusing series of transactions, wrongly thought she was the purchaser of a house and wrought certain improvements to it. She was held entitled on principle to a lien on it to the extent of those improvements[52].

---

[44] E.g. *Walter v. James* (1871) L.R. 6 Ex. 124.

[45] (1857) 2 H & N 564 (actually about acceptance of goods, but similar principles apply).

[46] But *cf* the difficult case of *Upton-on-Severn RDC v. Powell* [1942] 1 All E.R. 220, criticised at para. 14–04 below.

[47] *Owen v. Tate* [1976] Q.B. 402. (This case did not in fact involve a payment by mistake: but it is submitted that the principle in it applies equally to such payments).

[48] For possible reasons see Chapter 5 on 'free acceptance'.

[49] *Cf Greenwood v. Bennett* [1973] Q.B. 195, below.

[50] (1858) 25 Beav. 72.

[51] [1972] 2 All E.R. 800. See esp. pp.804–5.

[52] In fact her claim was defeated because of countervailing benefits she herself had received. It is also doubtful whether there was genuine acquiescence, since it is not clear whether or not the owner of the house shared the claimant's mistake. If so, then on principle her acquiescence should not have been effective.

Estoppel cases

In fact, however, claims of this sort are of comparatively little   3-21
importance, owing to the existence of the related doctrine of equitable
estoppel, which covers much the same ground[53]. Assume you wrongly
believe you have, or will have, an interest in my property, and as a result
of that belief you improve that property or otherwise alter your position;
assume further that I acquiesce in your doing so. (A typical modern
example is where you are my cohabitee, and believing you have an
interest in our joint home, you contribute towards extending it[54]). An
equity arises in your favour, which according to the facts may entitle you
to the full interest you hoped for or thought you had, or such lesser
interest (such as a lien for expenditure) as amounts to the minimum
necessary to do justice between you and me[55]. In practice this covers
much the same ground as the previous head of recovery; indeed, it is
rather wider, since it covers disappointment as to what may happen in the
future as well as traditional mistake[56]. However, it is not really a
restitutionary claim, since (a) it does not depend on benefit to the other
party – indeed, mere expenditure may trigger it, whether or not it
benefits anyone[57] – and (b) while on the facts the equitable remedy may
be equal to the benefit received, there is no requirement that it must be:
it may be either greater or less according to the circumstances.

In any case, these cases of free acceptance and acquiescence are not
really an exception to the general rule. In them, the plaintiff gets a
remedy not because he was mistaken, but because the defendant accepted
what he had done (indeed, the plaintiff need not have been mistaken at
all, though he often will have been). They therefore really belong in
Chapter 5 below, on 'Free Acceptance'.

A further exception? Mistake and the concept of 'incontrovertible benefit'

The principle against forced exchange that lies behind cases like *Falcke v.*   3-22
Scottish Imperial Assurance Co.[58] is understandably a powerful one in the
law of restitution. However, in one case it loses a good deal of its force.

---

[53] I.e. the doctrine stemming from such cases as *Dillwyn v. Llewellyn* (1862) 4 De G F & J 517
and *Ramsden v. Dyson* (1866) L.R. 1 H.L. 129.

[54] E.g. *Pascoe v. Turner* [1979] 2 All E.R. 945.

[55] *Pascoe v. Turner*, above.

[56] As in *Ramsden v. Dyson* itself. The plaintiffs improved properties belonging to the defendants
in the belief, not that they were the owners, but that if they did so they would be granted long
leases. See Birks, *Introduction to the Law of Restitution*, p.277 ff.

[57] *Crabb v. Arun D.C.* [1976] Ch. 179 is a good example of estoppel where no benefit to the
other party was shown.

[58] (1886) 34 Ch. D. 234.

This is where the exchange is one that the defendant would have made anyway even if not forced to make it with the plaintiff: i.e. where it is clear that he would have voluntarily obtained and paid for the benefit concerned even if the plaintiff himself had not provided it. In *Goff & Jones* terms, this is the case of 'incontrovertible benefit'[59]. Although there is no clear authority that a showing of 'incontrovertible benefit' will *generally* defeat a defence based on forced exchange, there are a few specific instances of recovery for mistake that are difficult to explain except as cases of incontrovertible benefit.

For example, a series of early cases[60] establishes that the *bona fide* miner of minerals which in fact belong to another (e.g. because his excavations inadvertently cross his neighbour's boundary), while he must pay for what he has taken, can if sued for conversion claim credit for the cost of extraction. Again, there is the difficult case of *Greenwood v. Bennett*[61], where it was held that where a *bona fide* purchaser of a stolen chattel is sued for conversion, he can at common law set off the value of any improvements he has made to it in the belief that he owned it[62]. Admittedly, these cases are interstitial, and both involve merely passive recovery, i.e. by merely allowing a defendant a set-off in respect of the plaintiff's enrichment[63]. It remains to be seen whether these cases will be extended to other mistaken renderers of unaccepted services[64].

6   THE PROBLEM OF MISTAKE OF LAW

3-23   Mistake of fact is an independent ground for restitution for money paid, and (more problematically) for property transferred and services rendered. By contrast, it seems mistake of law will not, without more, found restitutionary recovery[65], at least in the case of payments of

---

[59] Goff & Jones, *The Law of Restitution*, 3rd ed., p.19 ff. The concept is discussed further in Chapter 14 below.

[60] *Martin v. Porter* (1839) 5 M & W 351; *Wood v. Morewood* (1841) 3 Q.B. 440n; see too the Scottish case of *Livingston v. Rawyards Coal Co.* (1880) 5 App. Cas. 25.

[61] [1973] Q.B. 195.

[62] The principle is now statutory: Torts (Interference with Goods) Act 1977, s. 6.

[63] Though Lord Denning MR suggested in *Greenwood v. Bennett* that in suitable cases, e.g. where the owner got his property back *in specie*, an 'active' claim might also lie.

[64] See too *Craven-Ellis v. Canons Ltd.* [1935] 2 K.B. 403 and *Marston Construction Ltd. v. Kiglass Ltd.* (1989) 46 Build L.R. 109; in the latter case the existence of a principle of 'incontrovertible benefit' was accepted by the court. However, in both cases it is arguable that the services were in fact accepted, so the question was not directly raised.

[65] *Bilbie v. Lumley* (1802) 2 East 469; *Brisbane v. Dacres* (1913) 5 Taunt 143; *National Pari-Mutuel v. R* (1930) 47 T.L.R. 110.

money[66]. This rule has been rightly criticised[67], and the authority for it is weaker than might be thought[68]; furthermore, Australian and Canadian courts have declined to apply it[69]. Nevertheless, it was accepted by all members of the Court of Appeal in *Woolwich Building Society v. I.R.C. (No 2)*[70] that only the House of Lords can now change it. The House of Lords on appeal left the point open[71].

Nevertheless, this anomaly is in practice not very significant, for several reasons.

3-24

First, mistake of law is narrowly defined. For instance, a belief as to ownership of property or other private right apparently counts as a mistake of fact for these purposes even though founded on a legal misapprehension[72], as does a mistake about how the law is to be applied to particular facts (e.g. whether premises are so configured as to come within rent control legislation)[73]. Again, foreign law is always regarded as a matter of fact, so mistakes about it equally count as factual.

Secondly, in a large proportion of 'mistake of law' cases, there will in practice be some independent ground to refuse recovery. In the nature of things, many payments under mistake of law will have been made in submission to actual or threatened legal proceedings[74], or by way of compromise of an honest claim[75], in which case there can be no recovery anyway: yet others will have taken the form of mistaken payments of taxes or duties, where recovery is normally governed by specific statutory provisions and not by the common law.

Thirdly, mistake of law may co-exist with other independent grounds for restitution, in which case it will not preclude recovery. For instance, in *Woolwich Building Society v. I.R.C. (No 2)*[76] the House of Lords, in holding that taxes paid where they were not in fact exigible were recoverable by the taxpayer at common law, made it clear that the mere

---

[66] Which has been the point at issue in most, if not all, of the cases on the subject. There is no authority on whether (for instance) acquiescence in improvements to one's property made under a mistake of law can ground recovery.

[67] Not least by the Law Commission: see its *Consultation Paper* No. 120.

[68] See Goff & Jones, *The Law of Restitution*, 3rd ed., 117 ff.

[69] Australia: *David Securities v. CBA* (1992) 175 C.L.R. 353. Canada: *Air Canada v. British Columbia* (1989) 59 D.L.R. (4th) 161.

[70] [1991] 4 All E.R. 577.

[71] See [1992] 3 All E.R. 737. In fact no mistake of law was involved, so the point was *obiter* anyway.

[72] Cf *Cooper v. Phibbs* (1867) L.R. 2 H.L. 149.

[73] Cf *Solle v. Butcher* [1950] 1 K.B. 671 (a contract case).

[74] E.g. *William Whiteley v. R* (1909) 101 L.T. 741; and indeed (arguably) in *Bilbie v. Lumley* itself.

[75] See e.g. *Bullingdon v. Oxford Corp'n* [1936] 3 All E.R. 875.

[76] [1992] 3 All E.R. 737.

fact that such payments might have resulted from a mistake of law did not prevent their recovery. Again, *ultra vires* payments made by the Crown or any other corporation are recoverable as such, whether or not they also happen to have been made under a mistake of law.

Fourthly, the rule is mitigated by a number of exceptions. The main ones are these:

• If the mistake of law is due to the payee's deliberate (or conceivably negligent) misrepresentation of law, it is recoverable[77].

• Where personal representatives pay money as a result of a mistake of law, the beneficiaries may recover it from the recipients[78]. It is unclear whether this rule extends to payments by trustees in general.

• In certain cases officers of the court must repay monies received by mistake of law[79].

• For obvious reasons, payments made, whether by parties to litigation or by the Court itself, pursuant to judgments later reversed are recoverable.

7 EXCEPTIONS TO RECOVERY FOR MISTAKE

3-25   Besides the general defences to restitutionary claims, such as change of position (dealt with in Chapter 15), there are a number of specific points arising particularly in connection with mistake.

Risk

3-26   It must be possible for a potential claimant to take the risk of a given mistake, thus effectively waiving any claim to recovery. Imagine, for instance, that, induced by the belief that you have got a place at university, I give you £1,000; but I say at the same time that even if a clerical mistake has been made and you have not been admitted, you can keep the money. I cannot have a claim for restitution. Agreement to accept the risk may presumably also be implied: and it is suggested that, in practice, there will be many cases where the only reasonable interpretation of a transaction will be that the person rendering the benefit took the risk of a given mistake. You ask me for a book of negligible market value; I give it to you, not knowing that you have found an eccentric collector willing to pay £1,000 for it. It is submitted that I have (and should have) no claim against you: this is one of the risks

---

[77] E.g. *Harse v. Pearl Life Assurance Co.* [1904] 1 K.B. 558.

[78] *Re Diplock* [1948] Ch. 465.

[79] E.g. *Ex. p. James* (1874) 9 Ch. App. 609.

that a donor takes[80]. Again, suppose a bank honours a cheque having forgotten, not that it has been stopped, but that the drawer has insufficient funds to cover it. Can the bank recover the amount from the payee? Clearly not[81]: on a proper interpretation the bank is deemed to have taken the risk of this sort of mistake.

Compromise

Most payments to compromise claims involve no mistake anyway. You claim I owe you £1,000; I think your claim is bad, but pay you £500 to get rid of it; I cannot claim I was mistaken about anything. But this is not always so. Suppose I think your claim is in fact good: even so, I may in practice be able to induce you to compromise it for, say, 90% of its value. Nevertheless, it is suggested that I cannot recover my payment even if I later discover that I had a good defence[82].

3-27

Benefits rendered in the face of litigation

There is a rule grounded in public policy that payment made (or other benefit rendered) in the face of litigation cannot form the subject of restitutionary recovery even though the claim later turns out to have been ill-founded: the defendant cannot, as it were, have two bites at the cherry[83]. As has been seen above, this principle explains at least some of the authorities supposedly preventing recovery in respect of mistakes of law.

3-28

---

[80] Alternatively this could be regarded as a case of donative intent: see Chapter 15 below.

[81] See *National Westminster Bank v. Barclays Bank* [1974] 3 All E.R. 834, 841 (Kerr J).

[82] *Cf Cooke v. Wright* (1861) 1 B. & S. 559; *The Ypatia Halcaussi* [1985] 2 Lloyds Rep. 364.

[83] E.g. *Moore v. Fulham Vestry* [1895] 1 Q.B. 399; *William Whiteley v. R* (1909) 101 L.T. 741 (the latter also involving mistake of law).

CHAPTER 4

DURESS AND SIMILAR DOCTRINES

Some means of coercing others to do what one wants are justifiable; **4-01**
others are not. Not surprisingly, the recovery of benefits rendered as a
result of pressure of the latter sort is a well-established head of restitution.

Moreover, unlike the case of mistake, it does not seem to matter what
form the benefit takes, except in the form of the remedy given. Although
most of the cases concern actions for repayment of money, there is little
doubt that if you force me at gunpoint to paint your house or hand over
my car to you, I have an analogous right to reimbursement, either in
money or *in specie*.

This chapter deals broadly with two doctrines: the doctrine of duress
proper, which deals with unlawful threats, and then equitable principles
such as undue influence which serve to supplement it. Following the
scheme of this book, this chapter will not deal with claims for the return
of benefits conferred pursuant to a contract later impugned for duress or
undue influence. This subject raises special issues, and will be covered in
Chapter 6 below.

1 BENEFITS RENDERED UNDER DURESS

Forms of duress

Duress can be divided into two forms: (1) direct unlawful violence to **4-02**
the person; (2) other unlawful pressure. This does not mean that there
can never be restitution for other forms of pressure which are not
unlawful: but these are dealt with under separate doctrines such as that of
undue influence, covered below.

Direct violence

Money paid wholly, or partly[1], as a result of violence or the threat of **4-03**
it[2] is recoverable as money had and received. Chattels so transferred can

---

[1] *Barton v. Armstrong* [1976] A.C. 104 (in fact a claim to set aside a contract, but the principle is the same).

[2] Including, presumably, violence to a third party: it would be odd if a bank could not recover money paid to a robber who threatened to shoot an innocent but unconnected hostage.

doubtless be recovered by suing in conversion, since presumably no property at all passes. Analogous restitutionary recovery is available in respect of other property, such as land or choses in action, which is not transferable by mere delivery, and in respect of services rendered: details of the remedies appear below.

Other unlawful pressure ('Economic duress')

4-04   There is old authority that money paid to obtain the release of goods wrongfully detained can be recovered as money had and received[3]. More recently, it has become clear that this is part of a more generalised rule: money is *prima facie* recoverable if paid to avert[4] the threat of any act wrongful *vis-à-vis* the payer, such as a tort[5] or breach of contract, whether or not the person making the threat believed it was lawful[6]. Thus in *The Atlantic Baron*[7], shipbuilders in breach of contract refused to deliver a vessel unless paid an extra 10% over the agreed price, whereupon the buyers complied. Mocatta J held that the buyers would have been able to recover the extra sum had they not subsequently affirmed the transaction. Again, in *The Universe Sentinel*[8] shipowners successfully recovered sums paid to a trade union organisation against the threat of tortious industrial action against the vessel. Presumably a similar result would follow where a threat of a breach of trust was used to extort money, though no doubt relief here would be based on general equitable principles, such as that a trustee cannot profit from his trust[9], or the doctrine of fraud on a power[10].

4-05   To come under the head of duress, the threat must be unlawful. Thus, although the claimants succeeded in *The Universe Sentinel*[11], it was made clear that they would have failed had the industrial action been protected under the industrial relations legislation then in force so as to prevent it being tortious. It is less clear, however, whether it must necessarily be unlawful *as against the payer* in the sense that the latter would have a cause of action for damages in respect of it. There are good reasons not to insist

---

3   *Astley v. Reynolds* (1731) 2 Strange 915.

4   Or, no doubt, partly to avert: see the analogy of direct force, above.

5   *Astley v. Reynolds*, above (conversion): *The Universe Sentinel* [1982] 2 All E.R. 67 (inducement of breach of contract).

6   But honest belief may be relevant to any defence of compromise: e.g. *Moyes & Groves v. Radiation (NZ) Ltd.* [1982] 1 N.Z.L.R. 368 (semble).

7   [1978] 3 All E.R. 1170. See too *The Siboen and The Sibotre* [1976] 1 Lloyds Rep. 293; and *cf D & C Builders v. Rees* [1966] 2 Q.B. 617 (release of debt ineffective when it resulted from a blatant threat of breach of contract).

8   [1982] 2 All E.R. 67.

9   See para. 11-16 ff below.

10   Snell's *Equity*, 29th ed,, p.562,

11   [1982] 2 All E.R. 67.

strictly on such a requirement. Suppose you contract to supply goods to my private company: you then threaten to break that contract unless I personally pay you £1,000. It would seem excessively technical to deny my claim to restitution of the £1,000 merely because your contractual duty was owed to the company and not to me. This view receives some support from *Pao On v. Lau Yiu Long*[12]. A agreed to sell B Ltd. a given asset in exchange for shares to be issued by B Ltd. : A then refused to perform unless C, the majority shareholder in B Ltd. , entered into a certain guarantee. The Privy Council seemingly accepted that this could amount to duress, even though the threat was not against C personally (the claim in the event failed on the facts). Of course, this does not mean that *any* threat to commit a wrongful act against anybody will give rise to restitutionary recovery: there must presumably be some close connection between the payer and the victim of the threat such that the payer is likely to be directly affected by it. If my payment of £1,000 to you resulted from your threat to break a contract with some totally unconnected third party, my action would fail, either because my act would count as voluntary, or because of the principle of proportionality (on which see below).

One further point on unlawfulness. It is suggested that the mere fact that an act is criminal does not as such make it unlawful: there is no generalised right of restitution for criminal gains, any more than there is a generalised right of action in tort where such acts cause loss. The point arises in particular in connection with blackmail, where the threat to reveal the victim's past is criminal but not tortious: can the victim reclaim monies paid to the blackmailer? Despite certain unguarded *dicta* that blackmail amounts to duress[13], in no reported case has such an action succeeded on that basis: and (it is suggested) it is better to regard any right of recovery, if it exists at all, as based on undue influence or some similar doctrine[14].

There is little authority on property transferred or services rendered under economic duress: but it is suggested that analogous principles would apply here. To adapt the facts of *D & C Builders v. Rees*[15], assume that Rees had demanded, not that the builder release part of the price, but that he should carry out further work not required by the contract. It would be very odd if the builder did not have a restitutionary claim for the extra work.

---

[12] [1979] 3 All E.R. 65. Strictly speaking, this case concerned a claim to set aside a contract for duress and not to recover money; but the principle is the same.

[13] *Thorne v. Motor Trade Ass'n* [1937] A.C. 797, 821 ff (Lord Wright). See too *Hardie & Lane v. Chilton* [1928] 2 K.B. 306, where the same seems to have been assumed.

[14] *Cf Williams v. Bayley* (1866) L.R. 1 H.L. 200.

[15] [1966] 2 Q.B. 617.

Defences to duress claims

Waiver and ratification

4-06   One can always make a donation, even to a coercer. It is perfectly possible (though no doubt unlikely) for the victim of a street robbery to turn the other cheek and make a gift of his wallet to the robber: if he genuinely intended to do so, then even though in a sense the gift would not have been made but for the robber's threat, he cannot thereafter recover his property. This illustrates an important principle running through the law of duress: the restitutionary action is barred if the recipient of the benefit can show[16] that the victim intended to waive any right of recovery, or (which amounts to the same thing) 'close the transaction'. As Lord Reading put it in *Maskell v. Horner*[17]:

> "If a person with knowledge of the facts pays money, which he is not in law bound to pay, and in circumstances implying that he is paying it voluntarily to close the transaction, he cannot recover it. Such a payment is in law like a gift, and the transaction cannot thereafter be reopened."

The question whether such an intention is present is viewed objectively[18], and is simply a matter of evidence. The presence of a protest is neither necessary[19] nor sufficient[20] to negative such intent (though in practice cases will be rare where a person rendering a benefit under protest will be held to have rendered it voluntarily[21]). A declaration by the claimant that he acted voluntarily is of some evidential force, but for obvious reasons cannot be not conclusive: if extorted in the same way as the payment, it is not surprisingly just as ineffectual[22].

The right to restitutionary recovery may be negatived by subsequent ratification, as much as by an *animus donandi* at the time. This is neatly illustrated by the facts of *The Atlantic Baron*[23]. Some months before a ship under construction was due for delivery, the builders said they would not

---

[16]   *Quaere* as to the burden of proof. In *Mason v. N.S.W.* (1959) 102 C.L.R. 108 Windeyer J suggested that it was for the plaintiff to prove that his payment was not voluntary in this sense. But this seems excessively hard on the plaintiff.

[17]   [1915] 3 K.B. 106, 118.

[18]   In *The Atlantic Baron* [1978] 3 All E.R. 1170, the buyers were held to have ratified their payment despite a finding that they never subjectively intended to do so.

[19]   *Maskell v. Horner* [1915] 3 K.B. 106.

[20]   E.g. *Twyford v. Manchester Corp'n* [1946] Ch. 236.

[21]   *Twyford v. Manchester Corp'n* [1946] Ch. 236, where this happened, was regarded with some scepticism by Glidewell LJ in *Woolwich Building Society v. IRC*: see [1991] 4 All E.R. 577, 601.

[22]   See *The Universe Sentinel* [1982] 2 All E.R. 67, noted above, where the shipowners were forced, in addition to paying money, to sign a declaration that their payment was voluntary. They recovered nevertheless.

[23]   [1978] 3 All E.R. 1170. See too *The Siboen and The Sibotre* [1976] 1 Lloyds Rep. 293.

hand it over unless the owners increased their subsequent stage payments by 10% by the owners. The owners gave in and did so, but made no subsequent protest before they obtained the vessel. Mocatta J held that although the extra payments would originally have been recoverable, the owners' later inaction amounted to a ratification of the renegotiated transaction and negatived any restitutionary right of recovery.

Proportionality and reasonableness

If the benefit rendered is wholly disproportionate to the seriousness of the threat, it is suggested that recovery will be denied. To take an extreme, if unlikely, example, if I pay you £1,000 to persuade you to perform your contract to deliver some item of negligible value such as the morning milk, I should be denied recovery however wrongful your original threat. Put another way, if the victim could reasonably be expected to take some other course of action, he is expected to take it. Suppose, for example, you agree to paint my house next month; but some weeks before performance is due, you refuse to do so unless I pay you an extra 10% there and then. If it is reasonably possible for me to find an alternative painter in that period, it is submitted that I will be denied recovery. Again, suppose that the site owner under a building contract threatens to throw the builder off the site unless the latter does certain work which he denies is due. If there is a quick and easy means to settle the dispute, e.g. by an immediate arbitration, the builder might well be expected to use it, rather than doing the work and then attempting to claim the cost[24].   **4-07**

This principle receives at least inferential support from *The Atlantic Baron*[25]. There, Mocatta J clearly thought that had it been reasonable to expect the owners to take other steps, such as suing the yard for breach of contract, restitution could have been denied on that ground: and other courts, in granting recovery, have stressed the lack of any reasonable choice available to the claimant[26].

Benefits rendered under the threat of litigation

Benefits rendered in response to a demand backed by litigation, or the express or implied threat of it, are irrecoverable[27]. Traditionally explained on the basis that such benefits are 'voluntary', it is submitted that this is better regarded as a matter of public policy. Compromises should where   **4-08**

---

[24] *Cf* the Canadian case of *Peter Kiewit v. Eakins* [1960] S.C.R. 361.

[25] [1978] 3 All ER 1170.

[26] E.g. *Atlas v. Kafco* [1989] 1 All E.R. 641, 644; *The Alev* [1989] 1 Lloyds Rep. 138. See too *B & S Contracts v. VG Publications* [1984] I.C.R. 419.

[27] E.g. *Moore v. Fulham Vestry* [1895] 1 Q.B. 399; see too *William Whiteley v. R* (1909) 101 L.T. 741, *passim*.

possible be upheld; those who use the court's processes in good faith ought generally to be able to retain the fruits of their action unless deprived of them by the ordinary process of litigation.

As a principle of public policy, this rule is subject to exceptions. In particular, it is limited to litigation conducted in good faith; there is no reason to protect those who abuse the legal process by bringing claims they know to be bad[28]. And for constitutional reasons, it applies with less vigour to actions at common law for recovery of taxes and other imports paid to public authorities[29].

A further qualification? The problem of 'coercion of the will'

4-09   In *Pao On v. Lau Yiu Long*[30], it will be remembered, buyers of a property company executed a guarantee in favour of the sellers as a result of a threat by the latter to break their contract. Lord Scarman in the Privy Council denied relief[31], despite the wrongfulness of the threat, on the basis that duress requires a 'coercion of the will', and that the lower court had found no such coercion[32]. The buyer had merely taken a hard-headed commercial decision as to what was in his best interests; and having done so, he should be expected to abide by it.

This principle must, however, be regarded with some care. Any decision to pay money to avert the threat of a wrongful act is in one sense a commercial decision, since few people give in to threats unless they feel it is in their immediate interests to do so: but if this barred recovery as such, the law of duress would disappear. In practice, it is submitted that this does not really amount to a separate defence to restitution at all, and that all 'no coercion' cases are likely in practice to be cases where recovery is denied for other reasons such as waiver or disproportionality. The fundamental question is, and must remain, whether the pressure used was of the sort regarded by the law as legitimate[33]. Indeed, what seems to have swayed the court in *Pao On* itself was evidence that the buyers thought it most unlikely that the guarantee would in the event 'bite', and hence that they were happy to give it; i.e. that there was in fact an intent to give the guarantee 'in any event'[34].

---

28   E.g. the old case of *Duke de Cadaval v. Collins* (1836) 4 A & E 858.

29   *Woolwich Building Society v. IRC (No. 2)* [1992] 3 All E.R. 737; Chapter 13 below.

30   [1979] 3 All E.R. 65. Strictly speaking, this case concerned a claim to set aside a contract for duress and not to recover money; but the principle is the same. See too *The Proodos C* [1980] 2 Lloyds Rep. 390.

31   This was a contract case where the buyers sought to be relieved from an obligation, rather than restitution of money paid: but nothing turns on this.

32   See too *The Siboen* [1976] 1 Lloyds Rep. 293, 337 (Kerr J).

33   See *The Universe Sentinel* [1982] 2 All E.R. 67, 75-76 (Lord Diplock).

34   [1979] 3 All E.R. 65, 71-72.

2 OTHER FORMS OF PRESSURE

If only to keep one's terminology clear, it is best to limit 'duress' to threats to commit unlawful acts. This does not mean, of course, that other forms of pressure are incapable of grounding recovery. On many occasions they are, and it is to these we now turn.

4-10

3 UNDUE INFLUENCE

Undue influence is an equitable doctrine with protean characteristics. It is both a vitiating factor in contract, and independently of this a head of restitutionary recovery[35]; furthermore, it is a flexible concept that encompasses a hotch–potch of different sorts of coercion and inducement. Nevertheless, for the law of restitution, it can profitably be rationalised as involving the gaining of a benefit from two sorts of pressure. These are (1) threats to commit certain acts that, although not themselves unlawful, are frowned on by the law; and (2) the use and abuse of moral authority, whether actual or perceived. We deal with each in turn.

4-11

Threats and undue influence

Two kinds of threats in particular come under this head. One is threats to divulge information. There is normally[36] nothing unlawful in the blackmailer's disclosing unpalatable facts about his victim: nevertheless, it seems clear that money paid to avert this threat can be recovered[37].

4-12

The other head involves threats to invoke the criminal process. If you have stolen my money, I am of course free to prosecute you. It is probable that I can demand reasonable compensation from you by threatening to do so[38], and keep it if I get it. But I cannot demand compensation from anyone else: thus in *Williams v. Bayley*[39], a father who gave security to cover his son's defalcations when threatened with the latter's prosecution was successfully sued to have it returned. Similarly, it is suggested, if I demand more than reasonable compensation from you; if I do, you do not have to pay it and if you do pay it, you can recover it back.

---

[35] Hence many authorities referred to in this part will be contract cases.

[36] Though it may on occasion be a criminal offence, e.g. where the communication is caught by the Malicious Communications Act 1990.

[37] Assumed in, e.g., *Thorne v. Motor Trade Ass'n* [1937] A.C. 797, 821 ff. See too *Hardie & Lane v. Chilton* [1928] 2 K.B. 30.

[38] *Cf* Criminal Law Act 1967, s. 5.

[39] (1866) L.R. 1 H.L. 200. Also *Mutual Finance v. Wetton* [1937] 2 K.B. 389.

The thinking behind this is presumably based on a concept akin to abuse of rights. Whereas most rights in English private law are incapable of abuse in that they can be exercised for any (or no) reason[40], the right to disclose information and to invoke the criminal process are qualified in that they must not be used for extraneous purposes such as personal gain. It is unclear whether other rights will be thus characterised so as to give rise to restitutionary recovery in cases of misuse, but the possibility must remain open.

Moral authority and reliance

4-13   Assume I rely implicitly on your advice as to how to conduct my affairs; on your advice I then make a substantial gift to you (or provide some other benefit). If you can be shown actually to have misused your position to pressurise me into making the gift, it is recoverable in equity[41]. But the principle of undue influence goes a good deal further than this[42]. If I can prove that these circumstances of *de facto* reliance existed, I do not need positively to prove that you misused your position. It is up to you to justify your retention of the gift; and this you can only do if you can show it was independent and voluntary: that it was a 'spontaneous act of the donor' amounting to a 'free exercise of the donor's will'[43]. An example of this process at work comes in *Tate v. Williamson*[44], where on similar facts a sale at considerable undervalue to a confidential adviser was set aside.

4-14   Moreover, in certain cases the plaintiff's job is made yet easier. Certain specified relationships are presumed, until the contrary is shown, to put one party in a position of *de facto* reliance on the other. Transactions between such parties are thus presumptively tainted with abuse of moral authority without the need to prove actual reliance. Examples include solicitor and client[45], doctor and patient[46], priest and proselyte[47], trustee and beneficiary[48] and parent and child[49] (though not husband and

---

[40] *Bradford Corp'n v. Pickles* [1895] A.C. 587.

[41] E.g. *Bank of Credit and Commerce v. Aboody* (1988) [1992] 4 All E.R. 955 (overruled on other grounds by *CIBC Mortgages v. Pitt* [1993] 4 All E.R. 433; see below).

[42] The general position is usefully analysed by Lord Browne-Wilkinson in *Barclays Bank v. O'Brien* [1993] 4 All E.R. 417, 423.

[43] *Allcard v. Skinner* (1887) 36 Ch. D. 145, 171 (Cotton LJ).

[44] (1866) L.R. 2 Ch. App. 55. More recently, *Goldsworthy v. Brickell* [1987] 1 All E.R. 853.

[45] *Wright v. Carter* [1903] 1 Ch. 27.

[46] *Radcliffe v. Price* (1902) 18 T.L.R. 466.

[47] *Roche v. Sherrington* [1982] 1 W.L.R. 599.

[48] *Ellis v. Barker* (1871) L.R. 7 Ch. App. 104.

[49] *Lancashire Loans v. Black* [1934] 1 K.B. 380.

wife[50]). In such cases *prima facie* benefits rendered by one to the other can be recovered unless they are proved to have been rendered voluntarily and independently. But even here the rule is not absolute: the inference of reliance is rebuttable where the facts are sufficiently out of the ordinary to indicate that the presumption ought not to apply[51].

Defences to undue influence claims

Voluntariness and independent advice

Anyone, even if in a position to exert undue influence, can retain a benefit provided it was independently and voluntarily conferred on him. The burden of proof of voluntariness is on the recipient. Although this burden is traditionally discharged by showing that the claimant had the benefit of, or at least had been offered access to, independent advice[52], the essential matter is voluntariness, and the mere fact of independent advice is of itself neither necessary[53] nor sufficient[54]. As in the case of duress, subsequent ratification is also sufficient to bar recovery.

4-15

Lack of manifest detriment

In general the law of restitution is concerned not with loss to the plaintiff but gain to the defendant. It follows from this that, at least where the plaintiff proves actual undue influence (in the sense of actual misuse of a position of advantage), the transaction concerned can be undone and any benefit conferred under it recovered, whether or not the claimant actually lost out as a result. Thus in *CIBC Mortgages v. Pitt*[55] a wife was unfairly pressurised by her husband into mortgaging her interest in the matrimonial home to pay off an existing encumbrance and to buy a holiday home. Despite the bank's argument that the wife had suffered no obvious detriment as a result of the transaction, the House of Lords held that on principle she had the right to avoid the transaction (though in the event she failed because the mortgagee had no notice of the circumstances).

4-16

---

[50] *Midland Bank v. Shepherd* [1988] 3 All E.R. 17. But see *Barclays Bank v. O'Brien* [1993] 4 All E.R. 417, below.

[51] A clear, if recondite, example would be a prominent Chancery Q.C. to making a gift to his family solicitor.

[52] *Wright v. Carter* [1903] 1 Ch. 27.

[53] E.g. *Inche Noriah v. Shaik Allie Bin Omar* [1929] A.C. 127.

[54] E.g. where the independent adviser himself acts on inadequate information: *Wright v. Carter*, above.

[55] [1993] 4 All E.R. 433.

4-17   Anomalously, however, it seems that in cases where the plaintiff cannot positively prove undue influence and therefore has to rely on one of the presumptions above, the position is different. Here the transaction cannot be set aside unless the plaintiff can show in addition that as a result of it he is substantially worse off. This is the result of the House of Lords' decision in *National Westminster Bank v. Morgan*[56], where a wife, who relied implicitly on her husband to advise her in such matters, mortgaged her share in the matrimonial home to the bank to cover the debts of her husband's company. She nevertheless failed to set aside the transaction because her interest was already subject to an existing charge, which was admitted to be perfectly valid; this charge was to be re-financed by the new one.

She had therefore, in Lord Scarman's words, suffered no 'manifest detriment'. This result is understandable: the limits of the 'manifest detriment' principle are nevertheless unclear. In particular, there is no authority on whether the detriment must be financial. Suppose an elderly person, while under the undue influence of her solicitor, agrees to sell him at market value an *objet d'art* of large sentimental, but small pecuniary, value. There is much to be said for allowing her to undo this transaction, despite the decision in *Morgan*[57].

Litigation

4-18   The threat of litigation can no more amount to undue influence than to duress, and for the same reasons. This does not mean, however, that one party to litigation cannot come under the undue influence of the other on some independent ground: e.g. if the defendant to a claim asks the plaintiff's advice on what to do about it and makes it clear that he relies implicitly on his advice. In such a case any money paid in settlement would, it is suggested, be recoverable[58].

Laches, etc.

4-19   As an equitable doctrine, undue influence is subject to the usual equitable defences, including the doctrine of *laches*[59]. The so-called 'defence' of *bona fide* purchase is dealt with below.

---

[56] [1985] A.C. 686. See too *Bank of Credit & Commerce International v. Aboody* [1990] 1 Q.B. 923.

[57] Which itself might require reconsideration, according to Lord Browne-Wilkinson in *CIBC Mortgages v. Pitt* [1993] 4 All E.R. 433, 439-440.

[58] *Cf Horry v. Tate & Lyle* [1982] 2 Lloyds Rep. 417, setting aside a wholly inadequate settlement by a plaintiff in such circumstances.

[59] Which defeated the claim in, e.g., *Allcard v. Skinner* (1887) 36 Ch. D. 145, above.

4 DEMANDS CONTRARY TO ACT OF PARLIAMENT

The subject of public authority demands for more than is owing by   **4-20**
way of taxes or levies, or for services rendered under statutory powers[60],
and is dealt with in Chapter 13 below ('Restitution and Public Law').
However, in certain cases private suppliers of goods and services (e.g.
landlords and suppliers of electricity, gas or water) are affected by
legislation affecting the price thay can lawfully charge, whether by way of
overall maxima, or 'anti-discrimination' provisions, or by way of
outlawing certain kinds of charges. Normally legislation will provide for
the recovery of overcharges, and if it does it no doubt pre-empts any
right that may exist at common law. But if it does not, then *prima facie* it
seems there is a common-law right to reclaim any amounts paid in excess
of those allowed[61]. This right is a little difficult to classify, but seems best
treated as a form of statutory duress. The overcharging organisation is, as
it were, deemed by operation of law to be in a position to exercise undue
pressure on the citizen so as to justify recovery by the latter.

5 REMEDIES IN RESPECT OF BENEFITS RENDERED UNDER DURESS ETC.

Money paid

Money paid under duress proper, whether physical or economic, is   **4-21**
recoverable as money had and received, as is money paid under a demand
contrary to law (assuming recovery is available at common law at all).
This remedy is not, of course, available in respect of the equitable
doctrine of undue influence: nevertheless, it would seem that there is an
analogous personal right to re-imbursement arising here too[62]. If not, the
consequence would be bizarre; it would mean that if I made a gift of
£100 to you as a result of your undue influence and you immediately
spent it on ordinary living expenses[63], I would be left without remedy.

Apart from personal rights, there is the question of proprietary
remedies. In the case of undue influence there is (it is suggested) no doubt
that any sums transferred are subject to a constructive trust in the hands of

---

60   The so-called '*colorii officii*' cases.

61   E.g. *Great Western Ry v. Sutton* (1869) L.R. 4 H.L. 226; *cf South of Scotland Electricity Board v. BOC (No. 2)* [1959] 2 All E.R. 225.

62   *Cf* the Canadian decision in *Dusik v. Martin* (1985) 62 B.C.L.R. 1.

63   So as not to have the possibility of a defence of change of position.

the recipient. There is no English authority on whether duress (of either type) also gives rise to a constructive trust. But there seems no reason not to extend the analogy of *Chase Manhattan v. Israel-British Bank*[64] to cover such payments: if transfers rendered involuntary by mistake give rise to such a remedy, so also *a fortiori* should those affected by duress[65].

Property transferred

4-22   We can begin with physical duress. A chattel obtained by force remains the property of the victim; he can therefore recover it (or its value) by suing in conversion, and there is no need for a separate restitutionary action[66]. With other property (such as land or things in action), it is suggested that a transfer obtained by force will be void under the doctrine of *non est factum*, and hence that similarly no title passes.

What of economic duress? It is submitted that at common law this probably makes a transfer of property not void, but voidable at the election of the transferor[67]. In addition, it would seem that a constructive trust, if available in cases of money payments, should also be available here.

Apart from this, it is suggested that there is no reason why a personal claim in *quantum valebat* should not equally lie. If you coerce me into transferring my car to you, it hardly lies in your mouth to allege that you thought you would receive it free of charge, or that you have any reason not to be forced to pay for it.

Undue influence and voidable family transactions give rise in the orthodox way to a constructive trust, and possibly also to a money claim: see the previous paragraph.

Services rendered

4-23   It is suggested that services rendered under duress ought to give rise to a claim in *quantum meruit*, for the same reason as property transferred should create a *quantum valebat*: the services have been requested, and the

---

[64] [1979] 3 All E.R. 1025.

[65] In the case of demands contrary to law it was tentatively argued that these did engender a constructive trust: see the judgment of Nolan J in *Woolwich Building Society v. IRC (No. 2)* [1979] 1 W.L.R. 137. But the question did not have to be decided, and no answer was given.

[66] Though one may coincidentally be available: e.g., if a robber sells his booty and his victim chooses to waive the tort of conversion and sue him for the proceeds.

[67] There are *dicta* to this effect in the case of contracts affected by economic duress (e.g. *Pao On v. Lau Yiu Long* [1979] 3 All E.R. 65, 79 (Lord Scarman); *The Universe Sentinel* [1982] 2 All E.R. 67, 75 (Lord Diplock)). There seems no reason not to apply a similar rule by analogy to other transfers of property.

person who exercises duress should not be allowed to deny that they were rendered with the expectation of payment[68].

It is unclear whether, and if so how far, services that go to improve property ought to give the claimant an interest in the property. Assume you force me at gunpoint to improve your house: if you are insolvent, can I escape the consequences of your insolvency by claiming a lien on your house to the value of my improvements? Equity suggests I ought to be able to, either by analogy to the decisions on acquiesced-in improvements (e.g. *Unity Joint Stock Banking Co. v. King*[69]) or possibly by an extension of the doctrine of equitable estoppel.

Third parties

We have hitherto assumed that relief is sought against the person exerting duress himself. But how far is relief also available against third parties? As might be expected, the answer to this question depends on the nature of the claim, and in particular on what remedies are available in respect of it.

4-24

Where the claim is one for money had and received in respect of a payment made under duress - whether physical or economic - it is suggested that it should not matter whether the payee is the coercer or a third party[70]. If I threaten to break my contract with you unless you pay me £1,000, you can recover the £1,000; it should make no difference in this connection if I demand that the money be paid to a company controlled by me, and your claim is against that company[71]. The only exception, it is suggested, is where the payee is innocent and gives value: for instance, where X coerces me into paying X's debts to you. In such a case you as a *bona fide* purchaser ought to be able to hold on to the money[72], and my only claim should be against X[73].

If undue influence is involved, relief is available against third parties in two situations.

The first is where the recipient of the benefit is not a *bona fide* purchaser, so as to take free of equities: i.e. where he is a volunteer, or has

4-25

---

[68] Thus differentiating the case from that of mistake. Mistake is not necessarily induced by the recipient of services; duress, by contrast, normally is.

[69] (1858) 25 Beav. 72, See above, para. 3-20.

[70] Recovery under contracts avoided for duress raises different questions, and is excluded from this discussion. See Chapter 6 below.

[71] Presumably there would be a claim against me as well; the money was, after all, paid to my order although not to me personally.

[72] *Cf Barclays Bank v. W.J. Simms* (1979) 3 All E.R. 552, holding that where X paid Y's debts to Z by mistake, no action for restitution lay against Z. See too para. 15-08 below.

[73] Unless, presumably, X acted as your agent when he exerted the duress. Compare the cases on undue influence, below.

actual or constructive notice of the circumstances giving rise to undue influence[74]. It should be noted, moreover, that constructive notice in such cases is construed widely here. If the relationship between the actual parties to the transaction is such that one may well have exerted undue influence over the other, and this fact is known to the third party, then the third party will be affected by any such influence unless he shows that he himself took all reasonable care to make sure that the 'weaker' party was actually acting voluntarily. This is particularly significant where there is a close or familial relationship between the parties concerned, as shown by the House of Lords' decision in *Barclays Bank v. O'Brien*[75]. A wife mortgaged her share in the family home to the bank in order to guarantee the debts of her husband's business; she did so as a result of various misrepresentations[76] by the latter. The mortgage was set aside. The bank knew the parties were husband and wife but because it had not insisted on seeing the wife in the absence of her husband, warning her specifically of the nature of the transaction she was entering into, and recommending her to get independent advice, it was held not to have discharged the onus of taking reasonable care in the circumstances[77].

4-26   The second case where the third party will be affected is where the 'influencer' acted as their agent. Typically, this latter situation arose where a would-be mortgagee of a matrimonial home entrusted the husband with the task of obtaining his wife's concurrence to the transaction: it was always a nice question whether, on the evidence, the relation of principal and agent had been constituted between the lender and the husband, so as to 'infect' the lender with any undue influence exerted by the husband against the wife[78]. But, while this avenue of relief remains open, the Court of Appeal has recently suggested that the courts should not be too ready to find agency in such situations, at least where family relations are involved[79].

---

[74] See e.g. *Bainbrigge v. Brown* (1881) 18 Ch. D. 188.

[75] [1993] 4 All E.R. 417.

[76] Although the case actually concerned misrepresentation, the principles are the same as for undue incluence.

[77] Compare, however, *CIBC Mortgages v. Pitt* [1993] 4 All E.R. 433, where it was held that a joint loan to husband and wife for their joint benefit did not raise similar suspicions, and hence that the bank was not in the circumstances under the stringent duty imposed by *Barclays Bank v. O'Brien*.

[78] Compare *Kingsnorth Trust Ltd. v. Bell* [1986] 1 All E.R. 423 (agency found) with *Coldunell v. Gallon* [1986] Q.B. 1184, *Midland Bank v. Shepherd* [1988] 3 All E.R. 17 and *Bank of Credit & Commerce International v. Aboody* [1990] 1 Q.B. 923 (no agency).

[79] See *Barclays Bank v. O'Brien* [1992] 4 All E.R. 983, 1006-1007, 1013. It is suggested that the House of Lords' decision ([1993] 4 All E.R. 417) does not affect the statement in the text.

CHAPTER 5

FREE ACCEPTANCE

The concept of free acceptance has two functions in restitution. One is limiting: if the recipient of a benefit had no proper chance of rejecting it, this should make us think twice before making him pay for it (see, for instance, the approach to services rendered by mistake[1] or by reason of necessity[2]). The other, which is dealt with in this chapter, is positive: on occasion, the mere fact that I have supplied goods or services to you and you have accepted them gives me an independent right to restitution against you.

5-01

1 GENERAL

Assume you want to sue me for the price of goods or services provided without an express agreement between us. In many cases, there is no need to worry about restitutionary recovery; instead, the law simply implies a contract for reimbursement. If you send me a crate of whisky unasked with a bill enclosed and I drink it[3], or if I ask you to paint my house without discussing the price[4], the law has little difficulty in saying that I implicitly agree to pay you a reasonable sum.

5-02

But the contractual escape will not always work. We deal below[5] with the situation where goods or services are provided by way of incomplete performance of a contract; but there are other cases where similar difficulties arise. If I request you to pay X £100 on my account, it is clear I come under an obligation to reimburse you: but it is less clear whether that obligation is a contractual one. Again, suppose my shop window is shattered in a gale; you, a glazier, repair it while I look on and say nothing. Or imagine you are an architect in negotiation with me over proposed works: because I want to hurry things along, you at my request

---

[1]   See para. 3-18 ff above.

[2]   Para. 8-02 ff below.

[3]   As in, e.g., *Weatherby v. Banham* (1832) 5 C & P 228. We ignore the effect of the Unsolicited Goods and Services Act 1971 for these purposes.

[4]   *Cf Way v. Latilla* [1937] 3 All E.R. 759; *British Bank for Foreign Trade v. Novinex* [1949] 1 K.B. 623.

[5]   In Chapter 6.

prepare preliminary drawings; but then negotiations break down[6]. Acquiescence as such cannot create a contract[7]; nor can services rendered in an explicitly pre-contractual situation[8]. Nevertheless, in such cases I may well come under an obligation (based on the common law action of *quantum meruit* or *quantum valebat*) to pay you for what you have done – not in contract, but on the basis that I have accepted the benefit of it, whether by acquiescence or positive request.

5-03　　　Why have this head of liability at all? To say it satisfies your legitimate expectations begs the question: if the law provided (as it might, but in fact does not) that you rendered benefits to me at your own risk unless you took the trouble to extract from me a contractual promise to pay for them, you would have no legitimate expectation to fulfil. The best explanation seems to be simple commercial convenience, plus the fact that requiring request or free acceptance protects you from any prejudice[9].

One might think there was no point in distinguishing this from implied contract – if I am bound to pay, I will not care whether my obligation arises from promise or free acceptance. True: however, from your point of view it matters a great deal, and for an obvious reason. If you want to sue me for doing work badly or late, or for loss suffered because goods supplied were defective, mere acceptance will not do: you will have to show an actual contract between us[10].

2　REQUIREMENTS OF THE CAUSE OF ACTION

Acceptance

5-04　　　The clearest acceptance is a prior request: if I ask you to do something, I can hardly say I did not accept the benefit of it. Little more need be said about this, and indeed this is often regarded as part of contract rather than restitution.

5-05　　　Acquiescence, however, will also do – at least in some cases – even though it may be a good deal more equivocal than straightforward acceptance. If I watch you cleaning my windows and do not stop you, I

6　*Cf William Lacey (Hounslow) v. Davies* [1957] 1 W.L.R. 932.

7　The rule in *Felthouse v. Bindley* (1862) 11 C.B.N.S. 869.

8　*British Steel Corp'n v. Cleveland Bridge* [1984] 1 All E.R. 504

9　The argument over whether requested services benefit the recipient at all (Beatson, *Use and Abuse of Unjust Enrichment*, Ch. 2) seems, with respect, a sterile one. If they do, *cadit quaestio*; if they do not, the recipient, by accepting them, surely should be regarded as having disabled himself from taking the point.

10　For a neat illustration, see *British Steel Corp'n v. Cleveland Bridge* [1984] 1 All E.R. 504.

may well have to pay you; again, if you improve my house thinking it is yours and I, knowing this fact, stand by, you will get a commensurate interest in the house[11]). Now, at first sight this is difficult. You cannot impose a contract on me by saying you will assume that silence means acceptance[12]; why should you be allowed to impose restitutionary liability on me by similar means? The answer, it is suggested, is twofold. First, a claim for payment for actual benefits conferred is stronger than one to enforce a contract that may be wholly executory by suing you for non-acceptance: to that extent, it may be justifiable to relax the strict requirement of a positive acceptance. Secondly, injustice is unlikely in practice to result from such a relaxation, because in many cases – including most of the undeserving ones – an action for payment will fail for other reasons. Suppose you put a case of whisky on my doorstep unasked and I leave it there undrunk. The whisky remains yours, not mine; any claim by you for payment will fail *in limine* for lack of any benefit to base it on. Again, if you decide to paint my house without any apparent reason at all while I look on, I may well act reasonably in assuming that you are doing me a favour, in which case the third requirement – lack of gratuitous intent – will not be satisfied.

Furthermore, it is suggested that acquiescence is subject to a further inherent limitation not applicable to positive requests. To give rise to restitution, it must be interpretable to a reasonable bystander as acceptance not only of the benefit itself, but of an obligation to pay for it. This may be important; especially so, where you do something that benefits yourself but also happens incidentally to benefit me. Suppose, for example, there is an unsightly hoarding outside your house and mine, whose removal will raise the value of both properties. You tell me that you intend to remove it if and only if I pay my proportion of the cost, and that if I do nothing you will assume such acceptance[13]: I stand by, and watch you take it down. You should not have a claim against me; but why not? The reason, it is suggested, is that while my acquiescence in an action taken entirely for my benefit can reasonably be taken as comporting an obligation to pay, the same cannot (it is suggested) be said where the benefit to me is incidental to some advantage to you.

'Free' acceptance

As we suggested above, what justifies the principle of free acceptance is lack of prejudice to the defendant: if I accept that I am receiving   5-06

---

[11] E.g., *Unity Joint Stock Banking Co. v. King* (1858) 25 Beav. 72. See above, para. 3-20.

[12] *Felthouse v. Bindley* (1862) 11 C.B.N.S. 869

[13] Thus preventing me from saying I thought you were acting gratuitously.

something from you other than as a gift and then get it, I can hardly complain when asked to pay for it. But you cannot use this argument if my acceptance is due to mistake, or to other circumstances outside my control; if my acceptance is not deliberate and free, I may well suffer prejudice.

On the question of mistake, take the facts of *Boulton v. Jones*[14]. Jones ordered piping from one Brocklehurst; Boulton, who had bought Brocklehurst's business, supplied it and Jones (who had hoped to set off the price against money owed him by Brocklehurst) used it. Boulton's action in contract for the price was unsuccessful. It is suggested that an action in *quantum valebat* equally would (and should) have failed. True, Jones had accepted the piping: but he had done so as a result of a mistake, and his acceptance should not count for these purposes[15].

5–07   However, it is suggested that a mistake will not cause acceptance to be 'unfree' unless it caused the defendant to act as he did, i.e. unless he can show that, but for the mistake, he would not have accepted the benefit in question. The difficult case of *Craven-Ellis v. Canons*[16] illustrates the point. The plaintiff acted as a director of the defendant company under a contract of employment which, unknown to either party, turned out to be void because the directors who entered into it had not themselves been regularly appointed and thus could not bind the company to it. The company was held, nevertheless, to have accepted the services rendered, and to be liable to pay a reasonable sum for them. Although this is not entirely clear from the judgments, the reason would seem to be that if the company had known the contract was void, it would no doubt still have employed the plaintiff[17].

Acceptance may be equally ineffective where the defendant had no reasonable choice but to take the benefit. In *Forman & Co. v. The Liddesdale*[18] ship-repairers carried out work on a vessel that turned out to be unauthorised: the owners took the vessel back and later sold it. The repairers were denied recovery: granted that the owners had received a benefit, it was a benefit that they had had no reasonable opportunity to refuse.

---

[14] (1857) 2 H & N 564.

[15] But see, for the position where both the claimant and the defendant are mistaken, Chapter 3 on Mistake.

[16] [1936] 2 K.B. 403.

[17] It has been argued that *Craven-Ellis* cannot be a 'free acceptance' case at all because the invalidly appointed directors could no more accept Mr Craven-Ellis's services than they could contract for them. With respect, however, it is submitted that this would not prevent a claim against the company based on passive acquiescence. The result in the *Craven-Ellis* case was mentioned, and not dissented from, by the House of Lords in *Guinness plc. v. Saunders* [1990] 1 All E.R. 652. In any case, the problem would arguably not arise today: see Companies Act 1985, s. 285.

[18] [1900] A.C. 190. But *cf The Manila* [1988] 3 All E.R. 843.

Lack of gratuitous intent

We must be careful to prevent the principle of free acceptance turning   **5-08**
gifts into sales: if I accept a benefit from you thinking reasonably that you
do not intend to charge me for it, I ought to be protected from liability to
pay for it. Indeed, in practice this may well cut out many of the more
outrageous claims based on acquiescence. If you clean my windows for
me while I look on, a court may well be astute to infer that I reasonably
thought you were doing me a favour, or providing a free sample of work
in order to drum up future business.

Deciding when I should be entitled to assume a benefit rendered by
you is gratuitous is clearly tricky; in practice it will often depend on the
court's assessment of who should bear the risks inherent in a particular
transaction, and on any contractual or other arrangements between the
parties. We have already mentioned *Craven-Ellis v. Canons*[19], where
acceptance of services from an invalidly-appointed director were held to
give rise to a duty to pay. Contrast *Re Richmond Gate*[20], where the plaintiff
was employed by a company at such remuneration 'as the directors shall
determine'. No rate was ever set, and his action in *quantum meruit* failed:
his contract of employment excluded any right to be paid until the
amount was set, and up to then he was regarded as acting gratuitously.

Again, it may well be that the recipient of a given benefit is entitled to   **5-09**
assume it is gratuitous in some circumstances but not others. Suppose I
am negotiating to take a lease of your premises; in my impatience I ask
you to carry out improvements immediately; but then negotiations are
aborted. A court is likely to infer that the improvements were intended to
be gratuitous if the breakdown was your fault, but not otherwise[21]. Yet
again, often the real question is not whether benefits were to be paid for,
but who should pay; it may well be that a benefit was intended to be
gratuitous as against A but not as against B. A neat example is the
situation where I take my car to your garage to be repaired at the instance
of my insurers, but the insurers fail to pay. The repairs will be regarded as
gratuitous *vis-à-vis* me, but not the insurers[22].

---

[19]   [1936] 2 K.B. 403.

[20]   [1965] 1 W.L.R. 335. See too *Guinness plc. v. v Saunders* [1900] 1 All E.R. 652; where it
would be unlawful for a director to be paid for reasons of conflict of duty and interest, no *quantum
meruit* permissible.

[21]   *Cf Brewer St Investments v. Barclays Woollen Co.* [1954] 1 Q.B. 428.

[22]   *Brown & Davis v. Galbraith* [1972] 1 W.L.R. 997 (a contract case; but it is suggested that a
claim in *quantum meruit* would yield the same result).

CHAPTER 6

RESTITUTION AND CONTRACT

For obvious reasons, a great deal of restitution litigation arises out of contractual relations between the parties. True, as a matter of strict analysis, the essential issues are often the same in both contractual and non-contractual cases. For example, if I pay you £1,000 to do something, I should be able to get my money back if you do not do it. It should make no difference whether the £1,000 was for goods you wrongfully failed to supply (contract), or was a deposit paid under a non-binding agreement which was never performed (no contract[1]). Your enrichment is equally unjust in either case. Nevertheless, it is worth treating contractual restitution separately for several reasons.

6-01

First, a number of rules have grown up which are specific to restitutionary recovery between contracting parties. The most obvious examples are the working out of the common law rules relating to *quantum meruit* and *quantum valebat* in the context of partial performance, and the statutory provisions on frustration contained in the Law Reform (Frustrated Contracts) Act 1943.

Secondly, where a restitutionary claim is made against a contractual background, there may be a need to tailor relief so as to prevent it subverting the terms of the contract itself. For instance, if I perform services at your request without a contract, I should obviously be able to claim their reasonable value[2]: but if the services amounted to partial performance of a contract, then arguably I should be limited to a *pro rata* proportion of the agreed price for the whole. I should not be able to do better by performing in part than I would have done had I performed in full.

Thirdly, restitution in respect of contracts suffering from a vitiating factor cannot be discussed without some awareness of the general law of contract. Contract ousts restitution: there is nothing unjust about your retaining benefits rendered in performance of a valid contract. Take mistake: however mistakenly I may have conferred some benefit on you, if I did so in pursuance of a contract between us, then any restitutionary

---

[1] As in, e.g. *Chillingworth v. Esche* [1924] 1 Ch. 97 (deposit under agreement 'subject to contract' where contract never signed).

[2] *British Steel Corp. v. Cleveland Bridge & Engineering Co.* [1984] 1 All E.R. 504; Chapter 5 above.

claim must fail *in limine* unless the mistake was such as, under the general law of contract, would have sufficed to render the contract void or voidable. It is only then that the law of restitution will have anything to bite on.

1 RESTITUTION ARISING OUT OF VALID CONTRACTS

6-02   In nearly all cases here, we are concerned with one of two situations: (a) where money has been paid for goods or services which have not materialised; and (b) conversely, where one party has provided property or services in part[3] performance of the contract, for which he has not received the stipulated counter-performance (e.g. payment). Each calls for separate and extended treatment.

Money paid

6-03   One might have thought there was no need for restitution here: after all, if I pay you for a car which you do not deliver, I can simply claim damages for breach of contract. But a moment's thought shows this will not do. There may be no claim for damages at all (e.g. if you are protected by an exemption clause, or the contract was binding in honour only[4]); but I will still want my money back. Alternatively, a claim for damages may give me less than I want: if the car is worth less than the price agreed, I will get back less than I paid if I sue for damages.

The remedy here is the common law action for return of money paid for a consideration which has totally failed. This allows a person paying money to recover it in full if he can show that he has received no part of what was promised in return. It does not matter whether or not he also has an action in breach of contract which would yield him less. If I pay you £1,000 for a car worth £800 which you do not deliver, I can recover the full £1,000, despite the fact that the contract was a losing one. And rightly so: it is clearly unjust that you should be allowed to keep the profit (£200) that you would have made on the deal if you did not perform your part of it. Furthermore, it is equally irrelevant if the claimant himself is in breach of contract[5]; if I pay you in advance for

---

[3]   Obviously if full performance has been rendered, the claim is for the price agreed, and restitution does not come into it.

[4]   And equally in the case of a pre-contract deposit where no contract ever comes into being: *Chillingworth v. Esche* [1924] 1 Ch. 97.

[5]   *Dies v. British International Mining & Finance Corp'n* [1939] 1 K.B. 724. It is suggested that the contrary decision in *Thomas v. Brown* (1876) 1 Q.B.D. 714 is unsupportable.

goods but then wrongfully refuse to take delivery of them, that is no reason to allow you to keep the price (though you will no doubt have a counterclaim against me for any damage you have suffered).

Need for total failure

Restitutionary recovery here is limited to *total* failure of consideration: **6-04** if you get any part of what you paid for (e.g. if you pay me £500 to paint your house and I only do half the job), you are limited to your claim in damages, and have no separate remedy for a proportion of the sum paid[6].

This is a bizarre and unprepossessing limitation. The one argument in its favour, that quantification of partial claims might be difficult, is hardly convincing. A good deal of its sting is, in any case, removed in any case by the existence of a major exception: where a pre-paid seller of goods delivers short, the buyer is, exceptionally, entitled to recover the price pro rata in respect of what he did not get[7].

Collateral benefits

One further important point must be made concerning the need for **6-05** total failure. Receipt of anything *actually promised* bars an action for the return of money paid: receipt of some collateral benefit not so promised does not. Take the facts of *Rowland v. Divall*[8]. A bought a car from B, used it for some months, and then had to give it up to the true owner when it transpired that B had had no title to it in the first place. Despite his incidental benefit from use of the car, he recovered the price in full and was not limited to an action for damages, in which he would have had to give credit for such use.

This principle, at first sight odd, is more defensible than it looks. The seller does not have a strong claim to receive credit for a benefit to the buyer (use of the car) which he himself had no right to give. There is also a further argument. It is well established that a misperforming seller who delivers goods that are not in accordance with the contract of sale takes the risk of losses that occur before the contract is cancelled[9]. It is arguable that, by analogy, he ought equally to accept that benefits to the buyer are out of account[10].

---

6   E.g. *Hunt v. Silk* (1804) 5 East 449.

7   *Behrend v. Produce Brokers* [1920] 3 K.B. 530.

8   [1923] 2 K.B. 500. See too *Butterworth v. Kingsway Motors* [1954] 1 W.L.R. 1286.

9   The rule in *Head v. Tattersall* (1871) L.R. 7 Ex. 7.

10   There is a further point: the buyer in a *Rowland v. Divall* situation faces a theoretical liability to the true owner in conversion. True, he may well not be sued in practice: but if so, should this enure to his benefit or that of the seller? Surely the former.

Other possible claims

6-06   Where there is no contract involved, a person transferring money or
property for an unfulfilled purpose may (as we shall see[11]) have a claim
for its return based on resulting trust principles. It is tempting to argue for
the extension of this to contractual cases: if I pay you £10,000 for a car I
do not get, should I not have a proprietary claim to the money in your
hands? But this contention is misguided, since it fails to take account of
the need already adverted to adjust relief in contractual situation so as to
avoid subverting the contract itself. A person paying in advance for goods
or services presumptively relies on the seller's credit, and takes the risk
that it may fail. To put him in a better position by superadding a claim to
the money itself would therefore subvert the assumption underlying the
contract itself[12]: if he wants such a remedy, he ought to have to stipulate
specifically for it (as indeed he can[13]).

Goods provided and services rendered

6-07   Clearly a contractor who has only performed partly cannot claim the
whole contract sum: no-one should have to pay full price without
receiving full value[14]. Nevertheless, the common law of *quantum meruit*
(services) or *quantum valebat* (goods) may on occasion allow him a partial
remedy, to claim the value of what he has done. But this right is limited
as follows.

It clearly applies where the failure to render full performance is due to
breach of contract by the other side. If I agree to build you a house but
you wrongfully throw me off the site while I am building it, I can claim
the reasonable value of the work already done.

Equally, there is no doubt that it does not apply to benefit a claimant
who is himself in breach. A builder who walks off the site before he has
finished [15](or who does a job so lamentably defective as to be regarded as
incomplete[16]) forfeits – drastically – any right to recovery at all.

---

[11] See Chapter 7, below.

[12] See *Eldan Services v. Chandag Motors* [1990] 3 All E.R. 459, where Millett J refused an
injunction in respect of a prepayment to a seller, which would have prevented the seller from
disposing of the money.

[13] E.g. *Barclays Bank v. Quistclose Investments* [1970] A.C. 567; *Re Kayford Ltd*. (1975) 1 All E.R.
604.

[14] Unless the incompleteness is very small. 'Substantial performance', by an extension of the *de
minimis* principle, justifies a claim for the agreed price: e.g. *Hoenig v. Isaacs* [1952] 2 All E.R. 176.

[15] *Sumpter v. Hedges* [1898] 1 Q.B. 673.

[16] E.g. *Bolton v. Mahadeva* [1972] 1 W.L.R. 1009; *cf Hoenig v. Isaacs* [1952] 2 All E.R. 176.

Why the distinction? The most convincing basis, it is suggested, is the presumption against forced exchange[17]. A person buying goods or services expects full performance; he does not ask for, and probably does not want, anything less. It is therefore *prima facie* wrong to make him pay for it, however harsh this may seem *vis-à-vis* the seller. However, there is one important qualification to this reasoning. It is always open to a contractor to change his mind about what he will accept: and if, knowing that part performance is all that he will get, he chooses to accept it, the objection falls away[18]. This is precisely the case where the site owner wrongfully ejects the builder: it is his choice that he only gets part performance, and there is therefore no reason why he should not pay for it.

This reasoning explains a number of further cases.   6-08

First, the denial of recovery to a part performer in breach is modified in sales of goods where the buyer positively accepts the short delivery[19]. The buyer has the ability to reject what is offered and return it if he wants to[20]; if he chooses not to, then this undermines any potential objection based on forced exchange. Indeed, an analogous rule applies in other cases of part-performance[21]; though where services are involved it is likely in practice to be very difficult to show a genuine acceptance on the part of the other party[22].

Second, it may provide a clue to a situation not covered above; i.e. where the failure to render full performance is due to neither party's breach. Leaving aside the special case of frustration (dealt with below), what happens where the contract itself contains provisions allowing one or other party lawfully to put an end to it? It is suggested the answer should depend on who exercises such an option. If to the buyer of goods or services, there should be a claim: by exercising his right, he has deliberately chosen to be satisfied with only part of what he ordered. Not so, however, with the seller: there is no element of choice here on the buyer's part, and no reason to impose a duty on him to pay.

---

[17] See Chapter 14 below.

[18] *Cf* cases such as *Miles v. Wakefield M.B.C.* [1987] 1 All E.R. 1089 and *Wiluszynski v. Tower Hamlets BC* [1989] I.R.LIR. 259. See too para. 14-05 below.

[19] Sale of Goods Act 1979, s. 30(1).

[20] *Ibid.*

[21] See, e.g. *Miles v. Wakefield M.B.C.* [1987] 1 All E.R. 1089, 1099, *per* Lord Templeman (if employer of workers engaged in partial industrial action genuinely accepts the limited services they actually perform, liable to pay a *quantum meruit*).

[22] See once again *Miles*'s case itself, where no such acceptance was shown.

What amounts to 'benefit' under a contract?

6-09   In most cases of contractual restitution the defendant will have
tangibly received something from the claimant – a part delivery of goods,
an unfinished building. This is clearly a benefit, and the question is
essentially one of valuing it (of which more below). But not always.
Assume you agree to write me a book, or to sell me a picture having first
cleaned it; but before delivery of manuscript or picture is due I say I do
not want it. You may have a claim for breach of contract; but do you
have a claim for the writing or cleaning you have done? *Prima facie* the
answer is yes; witness *Planché v. Colburn*[23], where an author whose
commission was wrongfully countermanded when he had written an
appreciable amount recovered in *quantum meruit*.

Now, this looks odd: is not the author's claim really one for his own
time wasted (damages), rather than the publisher's benefit (restitution)? In
fact, however, the result is quite defensible. It is submitted that the element
of 'benefit' resides, not in any physical receipt of goods or services, but in
the fact of a request addressed to the person providing them. A couple of
examples can make this clear. Suppose, in the picture example, that no
formal contract of sale had been drawn up, but both parties confidently
thought it would be; the buyer, to save time, asked the seller to do the
cleaning immediately. If a contract was not signed, there is little doubt that
the seller could claim for the time spent: his services were asked for and
accepted by the buyer[24]. But if so, why deny such a claim where there is a
contract, subsequently broken? Again, change the facts of *Planché*'s case
slightly, and assume the manuscript was to be typed on the publisher's own
word processor, so as to be immediately available to him. It would be
peculiar, to say the least, that this should make all the difference to the
author's claim to a *quantum meruit* if the publisher reneges.

But the principle exemplified by *Planché v. Colburn* is of course only a
prima facie rule: it may be the common intent of the parties that payment
of any sort is only due on physical delivery. It is suggested that this
inference will readily be drawn in simple contracts for the sale of goods.
Suppose you wrongfully refuse to accept delivery of a vintage car which I
have agreed to sell to you and bring to your house. A restitutionary claim
for the cost of delivery is fanciful: my claim is in breach of contract or not
at all.

---

[23] (1831) 8 Bing 14.
[24] *Cf Brewer Street Investments v. Barclays Woollen Co.* [1954] 1 Q.B. 428.

Measure of recovery

The natural measure of restitutionary recovery for goods or services supplied is their reasonable value: but this may cause trouble in the contractual context in two cases.

6–10

First, what if the claimant has made a good bargain? You agree to build me a house on my land for £100,000: I wrongfully throw you off the site when it is half built. If the reasonable value of the work you have done is £60,000, should your claim nevertheless be capped at £50,000, representing the due proportion of the contract price? Subject to the problem of 'front-loading', dealt with below, it is suggested that it should be[25]. There is no justification for upsetting the terms of the contract as to price and awarding you a greater sum *pro rata* than the one you stipulated for: put another way, your agreement to do the work cheaply should preclude you from asserting that my enrichment from any part of it is greater than the due proportion of the agreed price[26].

What happens if, conversely, the value of the work done is less than the contract price (say £40,000)? Should the contract price preclude the recipient from denying that half a job was worth £50,000 to him? Although the point can be argued either way, it is tentatively suggested that it should not[27]. Restitutionary recovery is about actual benefits rendered, and while there is no reason why contract should not restrict restitutionary recovery, a person who wishes a more generous measure of recovery should be limited to his rights (if any) under the contract itself[28].

6–11

The second problem is the practical one of 'front-loading'. With fixed costs in account, a normal builder will charge a good deal more proportionately for half a house than for a whole one: should this be reflected in any restitutionary award, by awarding him more than 50% of the total price? There seems no reason why it should not: the customer, although the fixed costs thrown away did not enure directly to his benefit, ought to have known that they would have formed a larger element in half a house than a whole one, and that the price would have been accordingly higher.

---

[25] There is no English authority on this. In *Lodder v. Slowey* (1900) 20 N.Z.L.R. 321 a New Zealand court refused to cap the award; when the case went to the Privy Council the point was not discussed. See [1904] A.C. 442. For full discussion of American and other authorities, see Goff & Jones, *The Law of Restitution*, 3rd ed., pp.465–466.

[26] It should, of course, be different where no contract was entered into at all: there, there is no case for capping the award. See *Rover International v. Cannon Film Sales (No. 3)* [1989] 3 All E.R. 423, where the Court of Appeal reached this conclusion.

[27] But, in the context of sale of goods, see s. 30(1) of the Sale of Goods Act 1979, giving a part deliverer of goods the right to be paid for them at the contract rate.

[28] An action for breach of contract would presumably yield £50,000 for the work done. If there was no breach of contract, e.g. because of a power of termination, there seems no injustice in limiting the claim to £40,000.

2 VITIATED CONTRACTS

Mistake

6-12   It would have been easy enough for the law to provide that, once a contract had been successfully impugned for mistake, cross restitution for benefits conferred was available to both parties[29]. Unfortunately, it has not taken this logical course, instead leaving the subject to be dealt with piecemeal under the existing heads of recovery.

Indeed, the subject of restitution is made doubly difficult here, because mistake in contract is thought of by English lawyers in two entirely different senses. The first is where mistake by one or both parties prevents them reaching any valid agreement at all. The second is where there is a contract, *prima facie* effective, but one or other party has the right to set it aside on account of some error on his part[30]. In this second category one can also put contracts engendered by misrepresentation, since the issues are largely the same.

'No valid agreement' cases: Chattels transferred

6-13   A mistaken party who transfers chattels under a putative but non-existent contract has a right of recovery, but (slightly oddly) not a restitutionary one. Instead, the law provides that the validity of any transfer of title depends on the validity of the underlying contract. If there is no contract at all, it follows that no title is transferred, and hence the claimant can simply rely on his continuing property right. *Cundy v. Lindsay*[31] illustrates the point. A, masquerading as B, induced C to send goods to him on credit, which A then sold to D. C was held able to recover the goods by an action in conversion, not only against A[32], but against anyone else into whose hands they might have have come, including D. However pragmatic, this is hardly satisfactory: the effect on

---

[29] As effectively exists in the case of frustration (see below) and in the case of *ultra vires* contracts: see *Westdeutsche Landesbank v. London Borough of Islington, The Times*, 23 February 1993; para. 13-10 below.

[30] Or, if you prefer, the distinction between contracts void for mistake and those merely voidable.

[31] (1878) 3 App. Cas. 459.

[32] Note, however, that if A is innocent (e.g. if both A and C have been duped by a third party C) and A has disposed of the chattels without negligence, he escapes liability in conversion: *Elvin Powell v. Plummer Roddis* (1933) 50 T.L.R. 158. But this is due to the vagaries of the law of conversion rather than to any deep-seated restitutionary principle.

third parties is unfortunate, as is the lack of any of the defences, such as change of position, normally available against a restitution claimant.

(1) Other property

There is little authority on other forms of property transferred under non-existent contracts. Where the property is still in the hands of the transferee, there seems no reason not to allow the transferor to claim it under a constructive trust[33]. Claims for value, by contrast, are more difficult, since problems may arise over free acceptance. The issues are the same as those arising under services, dealt with below, and the reader is referred to the coverage there.

6-14

(2) Services

Suppose the plaintiffs in *Cundy v. Lindsay*[34] had been duped by the rogue Blenkarn into painting his house, rather than supplying goods to him. Or imagine that a fraudster X, purporting to act on my behalf, contracts to paint your house for £200; he then, as *soi-disant* agent for you, engages me to do the job for a realistic price of £500. I paint the house: you then discover the fraud, and X disappears. Can I claim against you for the value of my services?

6-15

Where the recipient has himself induced the mistake (i.e. the *Cundy v. Lindsay* situation), there should be no problem: it hardly lies in his mouth to say that he did not accept the services[35]. The situation is more difficult in cases such as the house-painting example, where neither party is responsible for the mistake; the services, while accepted, were accepted in error rather than freely. It is tentatively suggested that recovery should not be allowed here. True, it could be argued that you should have to pay £200, since although there was no agreement between us, *ex hypothesi* you were willing to pay that sum for the service concerned[36]; nevertheless, it is submitted that the presumption against forced exchange should prevail here[37].

---

[33] *A fortiori* to *Chase Manhattan v. Israel-British Bank* [1979] 3 All E.R. 1025.

[34] (1878) 3 App. Cas. 459.

[35] Indeed, in the *Cundy v. Lindsay* situation it seems clear that the rogue Blenkarn would have been liable to pay under the contract (*Mackie v. European Assurance* (1869) 21 L.T. 102): if so, no question of restitution arises.

[36] Particularly since, if in fact you had paid the fraudster X, presumably you would have a defence of change of position.

[37] *Cf* the discussion of *Upton-on-Severn RDC v. Powell* [1942] 1 All E.R. 220, para. 14-04 below.

(3) Money paid

6-16   Money paid pursuant to a contract that turns out to be non–existent is *prima facie* recoverable, at least where the claimant has got nothing in return. Thus in *Strickland v. Turner*[38], the buyer of an annuity got his money back when it transpired that the annuity had in fact expired prior to the sale: the consideration had totally failed. Where the claimant has got something, and hence the action based on total failure of consideration will not lie, the situation is not quite so clear. Assume, for instance, that in the house-painting example above, you were induced by X to pay me a £100 deposit before I carried out the work. Can you recover £100 from me? It is tentatively submitted that you can, despite having received the benefit of my services: the consideration for your payment was not simply the painting of your house, but the painting of your house *under the contract you thought you had entered into*. This has not happened, and hence that consideration has totally failed to materialise[39].

Other cases of mistake and misrepresentation

6-17   In practice, most cases of mistake and misrepresentation involve situations where there is sufficient agreement to give rise to a contract, but where that contract is voidable by one or other party at his option[40]. Restitution is less troublesome here, for two practical reasons. One is that where one or other party has rendered substantial benefits, such as services, which cannot be returned, the right to call off the deal will often be lost[41], so the question of restitutionary recovery becomes irrelevant. And secondly, even where one party is allowed to escape from the contract, terms may well be imposed on him to prevent him benefiting from any unreturnable benefit[42]. Since these are terms imposed by the court, as a condition of relief, there is no requirement that they fall in the recognised categories of restitutionary recovery.

(1) Chattels transferred

6-18   We have said that transfers of title to chattels depend on the validity of the contract under which they are transferred. Where that contract is subsequently avoided, any chattels transferred pursuant to it re-vest

---

[38] (1852) 7 Ex. 208.

[39] Compare the rule in *Rowland v. Divall*, that a mere incidental benefit will not bar an action for total failure.

[40] Either for misrepresentation or under the rule in *Solle v. Butcher* [1950] 1 K.B. 671.

[41] At least in the absence of fraudulent misrepresentation.

[42] As happened in *Solle v. Butcher* [1950] 1 K.B. 671 itself.

automatically in the transferor, who thus gets a *de facto* right to restitution[43].

This cannot, of course, apply where the goods have been consumed or destroyed[44]. This may give rise to problems where, despite such consumption or destruction, one or other party retains the right to avoid the contract. Suppose I agree to sell you 100 cases of champagne very cheaply as a result of an innocent misrepresentation by you: after I have delivered one case and you have drunk it, I discover my mistake and successfully avoid the contract. Can I sue you for the value of the champagne you drank? On the analogy of contracts void for mistake (see above), it would seem that I can. What if the sale had been at a high price, and you had sought to avoid the contract in reliance on a misrepresentation by me? Presumably my interests would be protected here by making any avoidance by you conditional on your paying me a reasonable amount for the odd case[45].

(2) Other property and services

The issues here are very much the same as those arising in respect of claims for the value of chattels, and it is thought that the results would be similar.

6–19

(3) Money paid

There is no problem where the person paying money under a contract subsequently avoided for mistake has received nothing in exchange: he simply recovers it as on a total failure of consideration[46]. Indeed, the same will apply even if he has received property: assuming he still has it, the effect of avoiding the contract for mistake will be to cause it to re-vest in the transferor, and there will still be a total failure. But what if the payer has received in exchange services, or something else that cannot be given back? The answer here lies in the fact that relief for mistake is not available as of right, and can be granted on terms: assuming the amount received is not such as to take away the right to avoid the

6–20

---

[43] See, for example, *Car & Universal Finance v. Caldwell* [1965] 1 [1965] 525. (But note the effect of s. 9 of the Factors Act 1889: *Newtons of Wembley v. Williams* [1965] 1 Q.B. 560).

[44] Where they have been sold to an innocent third party, no question arises, since here the latter's rights prevail: see e.g. *White v. Garden* (1851) 10 C.B. 919; *Lewis v. Averay* [1972] 1 Q.B. 198.

[45] *Cf O'Sullivan v. Management Agency* [1985] Q.B. 428, an analogous case dealing with services rendered under a contract later set aside for undue influence.

[46] Or, if the payee still has it, by asserting a constructive trust: *Chase Manhattan v. Israel-British Bank* [1979] 3 All E.R. 1025.

contract, there is no reason why the claimant should not be put on terms that he pay a reasonable sum for what he has got[47].

One further point. Occasionally a party to a contract will, under the terms of the transaction, confer benefits on, or become liable to confer benefits on, someone other than his co-contractor. For instance, if I buy a lease from you, I become liable to the lessor for rent. What happens where the contract is subsequently set aside for mistake or misrepresentation? The answer is pragmatic rather than principled: even though it is very difficult to say that such benefits went to enrich the other party, or even were requested by him, the person conferring them has a right to be indemnified by the other party[48].

Duress and undue influence

6-21   The definition of these concepts has already been dealt with in Chapter 4 above. Suffice it to say here that the forms of pressure that will suffice to allow restitutionary recovery in the absence of contract are the same as those which will allow a contract induced thereby to be attacked.

Undue influence and duress in general have the effect of rendering a contract voidable rather than void. This is clearly so with undue influence[49], and also with economic duress (e.g. where I coerce you into contracting with me by threatening a breach of contract or a tort[50]); the matter is slightly less clear in the case of threats of physical violence[51]. It would seem to follow from this that the rules of restitutionary recovery which apply where a contract has been successfully impugned for duress are the same as those obtaining in the case of contracts voidable for mistake and misrepresentation.

Frustration

6-22   At common law the rules on contractual restitution just outlined applied equally to contracts where continued performance was rendered impossible by frustration; thus there was in general no recovery in respect

---

[47] *Cf O'Sullivan v. Management Agency*, note 45 above.

[48] The rule in *Newbigging v. Adam* (1886) 34 Ch. D. 582. A similarly pragmatic principle applies in the case of frustrated contracts: Law Reform (Frustrated Contracts) Act 1943, s. 1(6).

[49] Hence the availability of bars to relief such as the rights of a bona fide purchaser.

[50] *Pao On v. Lau Yiu Long* [1979] 3 All E.R. 65, 78 (Lord Scarman); *The Atlantic Baron* [1978] 3 All E.R. 1170, 1182 (Mocatta J).

[51] In *Barton v. Armstrong* [1976] A.C. 104, 121 it was said that the contract was 'void' as against Armstrong, but no opinion was expressed as to its effect on the rights of third parties. It is suggested that a transfer in such circumstances should be void for all purposes. If the transfer is documentary, e.g. by deed, presumably the victim could establish voidness by pleading *non est factum*.

of partial performance[52], and money paid was, as elsewhere, recoverable only if there was a total failure of consideration[53]. The Law Reform (Frustrated Contracts) Act 1943, however, has since modified these rules and set up a largely self-contained code.

Money paid

Under s.1(2) of the 1943 Act, all money paid pursuant to a contract subsequently frustrated[54] is recoverable, whether or not the consideration has totally failed (thus reversing the common law). There is one qualification: if the payee has incurred expenses in performing the contract, he may be allowed to set them off against any repayment (see below).

6-23

It should be noted that claims under s.1(2) are limited to money paid to the other party to the contract. Money paid under the contract to third parties (e.g. where you agree to build me a house and I agree to pay your brother rather than you) is regarded as a 'valuable benefit' and dealt with under s.1(3), below.

Other benefits

Section 1(3) provides a generalised right of recovery in respect of 'valuable benefits' conferred by one party on the other, subject to a limited right in the recipient to deduct expenses incurred in or about the contract similar to that in s.1(2). A number of particular issues arise.

6-24

First, what counts as a 'valuable benefit'? Goods delivered clearly do: but what about services? *B.P. (Exploration) v. Hunt*[55] apparently distinguishes two types of service. Those without any tangible end product are valued as such: so, if I agree to provide security guards for your factory for a year and it burns down after two months, I confer a benefit on you of two months' security service. If a tangible result is contemplated, however, then – oddly enough – it is that, and not the labour that went into it, which matters. Hence in the *B.P.* case itself, where an agreement by B.P. to prospect and develop an oil-field was frustrated when the Libyan government expropriated it, the valuable benefit conferred by B.P. was the increase in value of the field plus any oil extracted by the concessionaire: it was not prospecting services as

---

[52] *Cutter v. Powell* (1795) 6 T.R. 320.

[53] Accepted in *Fibrosa Spolka Akcyjna v. Fairbairn Lawson* [1943] A.C. 32.

[54] If paid subsequently by a party who did not know of the frustrating event, it could not be recovered under s. 1(2), but could doubtless be recouped as money paid by mistake.

[55] [1982] 1 All E.R. 925.

such. It is not entirely clear why the Act here seems to go against the rule elsewhere in restitution, where benefits are generally valued as such[56].

6-25   Secondly, assuming there is a benefit, it is valued after, not before, the frustrating event[57]. This was held in the *B.P.* case to result from the wording of s.1(3)(b) of the 1943 Act, requiring the court, in remunerating a party for a valuable benefit conferred, to take into account 'the effect, in relation to the said benefit, of the circumstances giving rise to the frustration of the contract'. That provision, the court held, went to the actual valuation of the benefit, and not simply to the determination of the just sum to be awarded in respect of it. This obviously matters: thus in *B.P. v. Hunt*, the increased value of the concession due to B.P.'s exertions fell to be disregarded (except to the extent of the miserly compensation paid by the Libyans), since the concessionaire no longer had it.

Thirdly, as in the case of money paid, it may be possible for the recipient of the benefit to set off expenses incurred against any award made against him: see below.

Expenses

6-26   The law could have taken the view that, since a frustrated contract is a joint enterprise neutralised through no-one's fault, losses to either party should be split equitably. For better or worse it has not done so[58]; what it has done is take the more limited step of giving the court a discretion (if it considers it just to do so) to allow a set-off of expenses against a claim for money paid[59] or benefits conferred[60].

Despite the discretion given to the court, it has been said that this is in effect a statutory defence of change of position[61]. This factor, it is suggested, ought to guide any decision on how the discretion ought to be exercised to allow expenses. Suppose my contract to supply you with machinery is frustrated by illegality after you have paid me and I have incurred expense in manufacturing components. How much I can retain for expenses should depend on whether I can sell them elsewhere: to the

---

[56] Compare the common law rule in *Planché v. Colburn* (1831) 8 Bing 14, above.

[57] As, apparently, at common law: *cf Appleby v. Myers* (1867) L.R. 2 C.P. 651.

[58] For better, according to Stewart & Carter (1992) C.L.J. 66. *Cf* the British Columbia Frustrated Contracts Act 1974, s. 5(3).

[59] Including money that ought to have been paid before the frustrating event but was not: s. 1(2). The thinking is obvious: a party liable to make payment, but who has failed to do so, should not be allowed to take advantage of his own wrong.

[60] Thus leaving entirely unprotected a party who spends money on the contract before his co-contractor has provided anything in return.

[61] *BP (Exploration) v. Hunt* [1982] 1 All E.R. 925, 938 (Robert Goff J). For change of position generally, see Chapter 15 below.

extent that I can turn them into money, I have not really changed my position and should receive no credit.

Note further that, although a change of position defence, it is a somewhat restrictive one, being limited to expenditure 'in, or for the purpose of, the performance of the contract'. If, for example, I pay you part of the price of a house to be built by you and, before the contract is frustrated, you lose it in a disastrous investment, you cannot prevent me recovering in full, however much you may have altered your position in reliance on my payment[62].

---

[62]   *Quaere* whether you could rely on the more extensive general defence of change of position (below, Chapter 15). Presumably not: the provisions of the 1943 Act are no doubt intended to be exhaustive.

CHAPTER 7

CONDITIONS AND PRESUMPTIONS

1 CONDITIONS

Suppose A transfers property to B, but intends – or is deemed to have intended[1] – that the transfer shall not be absolute or without strings. For example, imagine I give you my car, but make it clear that the gift is conditional on your passing the Bar exams, which you do not. Alternatively, I settle shares on you as trustee, but die before I tell you who to hold on trust for. Some way has to be found to effectuate my intention, and to make sure that I (or someone claiming through me) gets back whatever was transferred, or its value.

7-01

Three particular cases will be dealt with here: (1) conditional gifts; (2) payments of money for particular purposes that are not fulfilled; and (3) gifts on trust that fail to exhaust the beneficial interest. It is true that at least some of them do not technically raise issues of restitutionary recovery at all. Assume I hand over my car to you, telling you that you can keep it if you pass the Bar exams this summer: but you fail. I can certainly get my car back from you: but this is simply because it has remained mine all along, and not for any reason of unjustified enrichment on your part. Nevertheless, there seems little point in excluding all such cases on such technical grounds, and they are therefore covered here for completeness's sake.

7-02

Conditional gifts and other transfers

A gift of chattels subject to a condition precedent passes no title unless and until the condition is fulfilled. If it is subject to a condition subsequent, any title is apparently divested on the happening of the condition, and the property can be recovered in an action in conversion[2].

7-03

What of other non-money gifts, such as land, or shares? With conditions precedent, the position seems to be the same as with chattels: a conveyance of Blackacre expressed to be conditional on the happening

7-04

---

[1] E.g. in the case of a presumed resulting trust: Snell's *Equity*, 29th ed., p.177 ff.

[2] E.g. *Jacobs v. Davis* [1917] 2 K.B. 532 (engagement ring: engagement subsequently broken off: successful action for return of ring).

of a given event will not take effect unless and until the condition is fulfilled. As for conditions subsequent, automatic revesting would seem impossible: the proper remedy here would seem to be a resulting (or possibly constructive) trust in favour of the donor in the event of its being satisfied. It is not clear whether there is a personal right to restitution in such circumstances as well: but it is, of course, always possible for A to confer some benefit on B expressly subject to a personal duty in B to pay A an equal or equivalent sum in certain circumstances[3]. However, such a right would, presumably, be contractual rather than restitutionary.

Payment of money for purpose not fulfilled

7-05   This has been dealt with in more detail in Chapter 6 on Restitution and Contract: but it may also be relevant here, since the action for money paid for a consideration that has totally failed applies whether or not there is, or ever was, a contract between the parties. So (for instance) it applies to money paid to a public authority under a putative contract which was in fact void as being *ultra vires* the authority[4], or the fact that one party thereto had no legal existence when he entered into it[5]. It equally applies, it is suggested, to conditional gifts. Suppose I give you £50,000 to give to X, but you fail to do so; again, suppose you are my son and I give you £50,000 towards the purchase of a house which you do not buy. In either case it is suggested that you owe me £50,000 as money had and received.

Indeed, in the latter example, if I made it clear that you were to use the actual £50,000 for no other purpose and were to keep it separate until you did so, I probably also have a claim that you should hold it on resulting trust for me, thus giving me a proprietary remedy and protecting me if you are insolvent[6].

A similar principle applies if I pay you money for a purpose that initially is satisfied, but later becomes impossible. I give you £100,000 to build yourself a house on Blackacre: if, once you have expended

---

3   Which will normally exclude any other restitutionary right in the circumstances – *Woolwich Building Society v. IRC (No. 2)* [1989] 1 W.L.R. 137 (Nolan J). But the Court of Appeal ([1991] 4 All E.R. 577) and the House of Lords ([1992] 3 All E.R. 737) found no evidence of any such agreement on the facts.

4   *Westdeutsche Landesbank v. London Borough of Islington, The Times*, 23 February 1993.

5   *Rover International v. Cannon Film Sales (No. 3)* [1989] 3 All E.R. 423 (unincorporated company).

6   *Barclays Bank v. Quistclose Investments* [1970] A.C. 567; *Re Kayford Ltd.* [1975] 1 All E.R. 604.

£40,000, further work is prohibited by order of the local authority[7], it is submitted that I can sue for the return of the other £60,000[8].

Failure to exhaust the beneficial interest

If the owner of Blackacre declares himself trustee of a life interest in it for X without saying what is to happen on X's death, he retains the interest in remainder: so also if I give property to you on trust, but die before I can declare the trusts you are to hold it on. So much is obvious, and indeed not strictly speaking a matter of restitutionary recovery at all: if I do not effectually dispose of my interest in property or the whole of it, I must as a matter of logic retain what I have not alienated[9]. The same reasoning applies even if I had no reason to know that I was not disposing of my whole interest. Assume I give my house to a charitable organisation for use as an old people's home, making it clear that I wish it to be used by that organisation and no other, and hence that the money is not irrevocably dedicated to charity[10]. If the organisation is later wound up I (or my estate) can recover the house. On the other hand, the courts are often willing to infer that a gift which might seem incomplete was in fact intended to divest the donor's interest entirely. For example, in *Re Andrew*[11] a gift on trust to educate the children of X was held, in the circumstances, to be intended as a gift to the children absolutely. It followed that the settlor retained no interest in it whatever.

7-06

2 PRESUMPTIONS

So far we have dealt with cases where it is clear that payments or transfers of property are intended to be conditional, or not to pass the whole beneficial interest to the transferee. In two cases this is presumed, however: (1) where A pays for property which is transferred wholly or partly into B's name, and (2) in certain cases where A gratuitously transfers money or property to B.

7-07

---

[7] Which would not amount to contractual frustration: there was no *contract* between us to frustrate in the first place.

[8] And, in suitable cases, have the remedy of a resulting trust in so far as the money is still in your hands: see note 6 above.

[9] Even if I did not in fact intend that result: *Vandervell v. IRC* [1967] 2 A.C. 291.

[10] Thus excluding its application *cy-près*.

[11] [1905] 2 Ch. 48. Another example is the well-known rule in *Lassence v. Tierney* (1849) 1 M & G 551, that if ineffective trusts are engrafted onto what would otherwise be an absolute gift, the gift presumptively takes effect unconditionally.

Payment cases

7-08   If I pay for a house which is conveyed into your name, one might have thought the law would assume a gift from me to you, and say that was an end of the matter. In fact it does not. Owing perhaps to the English habit of putting land into the name of one person when in fact several have contributed to the purchase price of it, the presumption is that the person putting up the money did not intend to make a gift, so that a resulting trust arises and the beneficial interest in the property is owned in proportion to the monies provided for its purchase[12]. In other words, since the finance provider did not intend to divest himself of his beneficial interest, a resulting trust arises in his favour. Hence the typical case: where a matrimonial home is bought from the joint savings of husband and wife but put in the name of the husband alone, the wife *prima facie* gets an interest in it proportionate to the amount she paid[13]. Similarly, if after the purchase the wife pays for improvements, she is deemed not to be making a gift but to intend to retain an interest in the property proportionate to the amount she put in.

7-09   Not surprisingly, the inference against a gift in such cases is subject to a number of exceptions.

It does not apply where a husband[14] pays for property conveyed to his wife or a father for property conveyed to his child, since here there is an equal and opposite 'presumption of advancement'. Accordingly, in such cases a positive case must be made out that no gift was intended[15].

7-10   It does not apply if a gift was intended: an inference likely to be drawn in the case of most purchases of personalty[16] for someone else. And, by similar reasoning, express provision made as to the beneficial interests in the property[17] concerned overrides any presumption and is given effect to *au pied de la lettre*[18]. Equally, if A provides B with money to purchase property by way of a loan, his right to recover the amount of the loan supersedes any claim by way of resulting trust. Contract here ousts restitution[19].

---

[12]   See Snell's *Equity*, 29th ed., 177 ff.

[13]   Whether paid by way of capital or subsequent mortgage instalments: *Burns v. Burns* [1984] 1 All E.R. 244 at pp.252, 265 (Fox and May LJJ).

[14]   Or, it seems, a fiancé: e.g. *Moate v. Moate* [1948] 2 All E.R. 486.

[15]   Which may not, at least in the case of a matrimonial home in present social conditions, be difficult.

[16]   But not all: e.g. *The Venture* [1908] P. 218 (a yacht).

[17]   Remember that most cases concern land, where there will of necessity be a formal conveyance. That conveyance will often spell out not only the legal title but also the beneficial interests taken: if it does, that is an end of the matter (see below).

[18]   At least in the absence of fraud or mistake: *Goodman v. Gallant* [1986] 1 All E.R. 311.

[19]   E.g. *Re Sharpe* [1980] 1 All E.R. 198, 201.

Gratuitous transfers

There is a weak presumption that if I gratuitously transfer personalty[20] to you I do not intend to transfer any more than a bare legal title, and hence beneficial ownership remains with me. But this very rarely applies in practice: the inference is inoperative where there is a presumption of advancement, and in other cases it is nearly always[21] possible to show a donative intent.

7-11

---

[20] Not realty since 1925: Law of Property Act 1925, s. 60(3); Snell's *Equity*, 29th ed., pp.182-183.

[21] Except in special cases: e.g. where a rich man transfers property into the name of his family trustees without specifying any beneficial interests (as effectively happened in *Vandervell v. IRC* [1967] 2 A.C. 291).

CHAPTER 8

NECESSITY

While away on holiday, you are taken ill and cannot get back home for some weeks. As your neighbour, I make the necessary arrangements and incur expenses to keep up your mortgage and insurance payments, repair burst pipes in your house, and so on. Or again: you lose your dog, whereupon I find it and feed it until reclaimed. Do I have a claim to reimbursement? That is the subject of this chapter. The main part deals with claims for necessitous intervention in general: the second with the specialised area of maritime salvage, which (as will be seen) is something of a law unto itself.

1 NECESSITOUS INTERVENTION IN GENERAL

Despite an instinctive feeling of sympathy for him, the *prima facie* reaction of English law to the necessitous intervener is to deny him recovery. However clearly beneficial his intervention was to the recipient, the rendering of emergency services in general does not give rise to a claim for payment[1] or any other relief[2].

Why? The traditional answer is that 'liabilities are not to be forced on people behind their backs any more than you can confer a benefit upon a man against his will'[3]; but this of itself will hardly do. One may understandably feel unwilling to reward the officious bystander who insists on rendering services to someone who, for all he knows, may not want them at all; but there is a world of difference between him and someone who, for good reason, confers a benefit which it is almost certain the recipient (a) would have wanted; and (b) would have obtained and doubtless paid for had he had the chance.

On the other hand, the present approach, which denies even the latter a remedy, may well be justified for another reason. In most other cases of restitution, the plaintiff has been able to show something more than mere benefit to the defendant, however incontrovertible: in particular, he can

---

[1] The question of maritime salvage is dealt with below.

[2] E.g. a lien: see *Nicholson v. Chapman* (1793) 2 H. Bl. 254 (feeding a lost animal); *Re Leslie* (1883) 23 Ch. D. 552, *Falcke v. Scottish Imperial Insurance* (1886) 34 Ch. D. 234 (payment of premiums to keep up insurance policy).

[3] *Falcke v. Scottish Imperial Insurance Co.* [1886] 34 Ch. D. 234, 248 (Bowen LJ).

normally demonstrate either or both of (a) a lack of voluntariness on his part (e.g. mistake, duress) in rendering the benefit, and (b) acceptance by the defendant – or at the very least, a rejected opportunity to decline it. In necessitous intervention, by contrast, neither of these is present. I do not have to help you in an emergency, and I know this: if I do, you have no choice whether to benefit from what I have done[4].

8-04   It follows that, in order to give a remedy here, we must find some way to relax either the need for involuntariness, or the requirement of free acceptance.

The first possibility effectively involves replacing 'involuntary' with the wider 'non-officious': meritorious claimants such as the necessitous intervener being able to satisfy the latter but not the former criterion. This obviously raises difficult issues of the place of officiousness in restitution law (i.e. should it merely be a bar to recovery that would otherwise be available, or should the lack of it in some cases be an independent ground for relief?). Suffice it to say here that, in the author's view, rewarding the necessitous intervener merely because he is non-officious overly undermines the principle that altruism should be its own reward. Voluntary transfers of wealth, however unmeritorious the recipient, should generally be allowed to lie where they fall.

Alternatively, one can argue that just as the person who receives a benefit willy-nilly from someone not acting voluntarily may be forced to pay for it if it was in fact 'incontrovertible', a similar rule should apply in the case of necessitous intervention. But this, it is submitted, seriously underplays the value of freedom of property and the principle against forced exchange[5]. Where the benefit is one the defendant never consented to receive, nor the plaintiff to give, the equities are, so to speak, equal, and a balancing claim may well be justified. But this cannot be so if the plaintiff acted voluntarily; however meritorious he was, and indeed even if he had a moral duty to do as he did, the fact remains that he did so out of choice, and there is no reason to upset the status quo.

2 THE EXCEPTIONS TO NON-RECOVERY

8-05   As might be expected, the principle outlined above is not an absolute one, and there are a number of exceptions to it. Although there is no general explanation that can justify them all, they tend to fall into two

---

[4] Of course in some cases of emergency intervention you do have an effective choice, for instance where I pay your debts in your name and you then ratify my acts: but then you can be held liable on free acceptance principles anyway.

[5] For fuller discussion of the supposed principle of 'incontrovertible benefit', see para. 14-09 ff below.

groups. First, there are the cases where the terms of some pre-existing relationship between the parties can be invoked so as to give rise to an obligation to pay for necessitous intervention[6]. Secondly, in a number of other instances recovery is allowed (it is suggested) largely on the basis of public policy, as with emergency medical attention or actions to save animals, or where some public duty of A's duty is in fact carried out by B in circumstances of urgency.

Pre-existing relationships

Agency of necessity

A number of cases[7] demonstrate that where an agent (often, but by no means necessarily, a carrier) is in possession of his principal's goods or otherwise conducting the principal's affairs and an emergency arises requiring immediate action, then, assuming it is impracticable to make contact with the principal, the agent is entitled to do whatever is necessary and charge the principal accordingly. The doctrinal basis for this is that the relation between principal and agent is deemed to include an implied term to this effect which comes into operation in the event of some unforeseen catastrophe[8]. It goes without saying that the doctrine may be excluded by agreement between principal and agent.

In practice, however, agency of necessity is not an easy principle to invoke. Most of the cases date from before the time of widespread instantaneous communication; today, it is likely to be rare in practice for an agent to be able to show that it was impossible to obtain proper instructions.

Bailment

By an analogous principle, it was held in *The Winson*[9] that a bailee of goods, in so far as he was under a duty to take steps to look after them[10],   8-06

---

[6] '... [I]n English law a mere stranger cannot compel an owner of goods to pay for a benefit bestowed upon him against his will; but this latter principle does not apply where there is a pre-existing legal relationship between the owner of the goods and the bestower of the benefit, such as that of bailor and bailee ...' - Lord Diplock in *The Winson* [1982] A.C. 939, 961.

[7] E.g. *Notara v. Henderson* (1872) L.R. 7 Q.B. 225; *Cargo ex Argos* (1873) L.R. 5 P.C. 134. See generally Bowstead, *Agency*, 15th ed., pp.84 ff.

[8] *Cf Gt Northern Ry v. Swaffield* (1874) L.R. 9 Ex. 132. A carrier fed and stabled a horse which the owner neglected to collect from it; Kelly CB held it was able to claim the costs incurred, on the basis of an implied contract.

[9] [1982] A.C. 939. See too *Gt Northern Ry v. Swaffield* (1874) L.R. 9 Ex. 132 (though the basis of this decision is unclear. It may have been a case of agency of necessity, above; or possibly a 'public policy' case: see below).

[10] But no further: [1982] A.C. 939, 960-961 (Lord Diplock).

could charge the bailor his reasonable costs of doing so. Hence salvors who took steps to preserve wheat after they had finished salving it from a stricken ship (having received no instructions from its owners as to what to do with it) successfully recovered their costs incurred in doing so.

This right of the bailee is distinct from agency of necessity, in that it applies in wider circumstances than those giving rise to agency of necessity[11]; however, it is submitted that it is likely in practice to be limited to emergency, rather than foreseen, preservative measures. If you ask me to look after your cat while you are away, no doubt I can charge you for emergency veterinary treatment if it becomes ill: on the other hand, it seems unlikely that, without specific agreement, you would become legally liable to pay me the cost of merely feeding it.

Trust

8-07

A trustee has no implied right to payment for acting as such. If the trust instrument provides for remuneration, he is normally limited to that stipulated; if it does not, he must act for nothing. Nevertheless, he has two specific ways of claiming for emergency measures connected with the trust estate.

First, he has the right to be re-imbursed any expenditure incurred in and about the administration of the trust, provided it is reasonable. There is little doubt that this would cover emergency expenditure such as (for instance) arranging for the preservation of a trust building damaged in a storm. Such a right is normally limited to the property forming the trust estate: but where all beneficiaries are *sui juris* they may be personally liable as well[12].

Secondly, the Court has inherent[13] jurisdiction to allow or increase remuneration in respect of extra work not contemplated when the trust was set up[14]. In a suitable case, there seems no reason why this should not be invoked to allow a trustee to claim for emergency services rendered personally[15].

---

11   Which was specifically negatived in *The Winson*, since it was not impossible to get into contact with the principal in that case.

12   See e.g., *Hardoon v. Belilios* [1901] A.C. 118; *Buchan v. Ayre* [1915] 2 Ch. 474.

13   And statutory: s. 57, Trustee Act 1925.

14   E.g. *Re Duke of Norfolk's S.T.* [1983] 1 All E.R. 220, and cases there cited.

15   And *cf Re Berkeley Applegate* [1988] 3 All E.R. 71 (liquidator of company holding assets on trust, though not trustee as such, has similar right of reimbursement against trust assets).

Other cases

Medical attention

In England, the problem of whether a patient should have to pay for   **8-08**
emergency medical attention has never had to be faced: but if such a
claim were brought it would probably fail. Restitution law has to take
account of surrounding social circumstances and, in a country where
medical attention is free for the asking even in the absence of an
emergency, it would be odd if the mere fact of an emergency made all
the difference. Put more formally, it would normally be inferred that such
services were rendered with donative intent, hence ousting any
restitutionary claim[16].

On the other hand, this is a feature peculiar to British society. The
problem has arisen elsewhere, and is worth discussing on the point of
principle. In the United States recovery is common, at least provided
there is no evidence that the doctor intended to act gratuitously[17], and in
Canada the leading case allowed recovery to a doctor who attempted
(unsuccessfully, as it turned out) to revive a suicide victim[18].

Why should this be, given that there is neither mistake by the doctor
nor an opportunity to reject in the patient? It is suggested that there are
two possible answers. One is simply ethical[19]; circumstances alter cases,
and the value of saving life is such as to justify special rules as to payment
and a dispensation from the normal rules circumscribing restitutionary
recovery. Alternatively, it could conceivably be argued that a doctor
intervening in an emergency, acts under practical, if not strictly legal,
compulsion, and hence should be entitled to recover by analogy to
anyone else forced to benefit the defendant[20]. It may not matter which
explanation is accepted, though the former seems more convincing[21].

If the doctor can recover, should it matter (a) that his services are
unsuccessful, or (b) that he acted against the will of the patient, as in the
case of a suicide victim? On (a), it is suggested that success should be
irrelevant. Had the patient had the opportunity of rejecting his services,

---

[16] See para. 15-04 ff below.

[17] See G. Palmer, *Law of Restitution*, §10.4 for the authorities.

[18] *Matheson v. Smiley* [1932] 2 D.L.R. 787.

[19] As arguably in the case of necessaries supplied to those who cannot otherwise contract at all: *cf*
Re Rhodes (1890) 44 Ch. D. 94, which indeed was cited by the Canadian court in *Matheson v.*
Smiley.

[20] See Chapter 9 below.

[21] It might also have the effect of allowing those who are not doctors, and who thus have no
professional duty to assist, to recover in suitable cases.

there is no doubt that they would have given rise to a claim whether or not successful[22]: if, as a matter of public policy, we dispense with the need to show acceptance, it is hard to see why this should make all the difference.

Point (b) is more difficult. On balance, however, it is suggested that restitution should not be granted if it is clear that the attention was positively unwanted: the fundamantal right to choose one's own destiny ought to override the undoubted arguments of policy in favour of recovery. On the other hand, the evidence should have to be clear: and there is no reason why the mere fact that (say) the defendant had tried to commit suicide should be conclusive.

Supply of necessaries to incompetents

8-09 This is not a problem that often arises. A mentally disordered person is liable on a contract except in so far as he is unable to understand the nature of the transaction[23], and even then if the other party does not know of his disability[24]. But if he is obviously incapable of any rational action action at all, he is nevertheless liable for necessaries supplied, presumably on similar ethical grounds to those above[25].

As regards minors, the law of contract once again normally provides a remedy: a minor is capable of agreeing to pay a reasonable sum[26] for necessaries supplied[27], and emergency services will nearly always be necessaries. Presumably as regards very young children a similar rule applies as with entirely irrational persons of unsound mind.

Animals

8-10 You omit to feed your dog; if I give it something to prevent it starving, can I claim for my time or expense? In *Gt Northern Ry v. Swaffield*[28] a claim of this sort was allowed; but this is hardly strong authority, since the plaintiff was a carrier and the defendant could clearly have been held liable on agency of necessity or bailment principles. Nevertheless, arguably the clear public policy against unnecessary suffering should dictate recovery even in the absence of a pre-existing relationship.

---

22 And *cf* the discussion of *Planché v. Colburn* (1831) 8 Bing 14, para. 6–09 above.

23 *Cf Re K* [1988] 1 All E.R. 358 (power of attorney).

24 *Hart v. O'Connor* [1985] A.C. 1000.

25 E.g. *West Ham Union v. Pearson* (1890) 62 L.T. 638; *cf Pontypridd Union v. Drew* [1927] 1 K.B. 214. But not where the person supplying the necessaries evinced a donative intent: *Re Rhodes* (1890) 44 Ch. D. 94. See generally para. 15–04 ff below.

26 *Pontypridd Union v. Drew* [1927] 1 K.B. 214, 220.

27 E.g. *Nash v. Inman* [1908] 2 K.B. 1.

28 (1874) L.R. 9 Ex. 132.

Even then, it is debatable whether this is really restitutionary recovery. Assuming a claim lies, it does so more on the basis of humanity than of benefit to the defendant. Suppose, for instance, that the owner of the animal expressly refused the claimant's services, or proved to the court's satisfaction that he had wished to abandon the animal to its fate and thus would not himself have incurred the expense of feeding it. On ordinary restitution principles this would defeat any claim for reimbursement; but it seems unlikely that it would defeat this one.

Public duties

It is clear law that if I am legally compelled to perform your public duty, I have a claim against you[29]. It would have been possible for the law to generalise from the 'public policy' cases and extend this principle to situations where my performance of your public duty was not forced, but was carried out reasonably in a case of urgent necessity. In *Macclesfield Corp. v. Gt Central Ry*[30], however, the Court of Appeal set its face against such a restitutionary *actio popularis*. A railway company responsible for maintaining a highway allowed it to get into dangerous disrepair. The local authority, having notified them of their duty to repair it with no effect, did the job itself. In the absence of proof that the authority was bound in law to do as it had done, its action for the costs incurred failed.

8–11

Nevertheless, there is authority for recovery in at least one case, albeit rather macabre: where those responsible for the burial of a dead body failed to carry out their responsibility, any other person who shouldered the responsibility was given a right of recovery against them[31]. This right seems to have been limited to cases where the intervention was not intended to be gratuitous, and where the intervening party had some reasonable excuse – such as a close relationship with the deceased – for interfering.

It is also worth mentioning in this connection that there are numerous statutory provisions giving equivalent rights to public authorities who carry out works, normally connected with health or safety: having carried them out, the authority is normally able to recover the cost from the owner or occupier concerned[32].

---

[29] E.g. *Gebhardt v. Saunders* [1892] 2 Q.B. 452 (lessee forced to abate statutory nuisance that was in fact lessor's responsibility).

[30] [1911] 2 K.B. 528

[31] E.g. *Jenkins v. Tucker* (1788) 1 H. Bl. 90; *Tugwell v. Heyman* (1812) 3 Camp. 298.

[32] See, for a random example, Highways Act 1980, s. 165(3) (removal of dangers to highway users by highway authority).

Acceptance for honour and bills of exchange

8-12   It has been argued that in at least one case, the necessitous intervener is rewarded even though he does not fall within any of these exceptions. Under s.65 of the Bills of Exchange Act 1882, where a bill has been dishonoured, it is open to any person to accept liability on it 'for the honour' of the drawer or acceptor: having done so and paid it, that person is by s.68(5) subrogated to any rights of the holder. But this is hardly a strong example. To begin with, while it is true that the acceptor for honour need not act at the request of the acceptor, he often will: and if he does, no question of liability for necessitous intervention pure and simple arises. More importantly, it is not only those who become parties to a bill in the case of necessity who gain the right to sue the acceptor: any indorser has a similar right, and indeed (it seems) anyone else who signs the bill other than as an indorser[33]. It is suggested that the best explanation for the rights of an acceptor for honour is the more prosaic one that bills of exchange are *sui generis*; when accepting a bill, one should know that others are likely to put their names to it and gain potential rights under it.

3   MARITIME SALVAGE

In general

8-13   In contrast to the position on land, the right of the maritime[34] salvor to remuneration is well established. It arises whenever a ship or cargo is, or reasonably seems to be, in danger[35], and is voluntarily saved by the efforts of those who are not bound by the terms of their employment or otherwise to do so. In practice a great deal of salvage today is carried out contractually, in particular under standard forms of contract such as Lloyds Open Form; nevertheless, the general rules remain important, since (a) the principles applicable under Lloyds Open Form are often similar to those that would apply even in the absence of contract; and (b) a substantial amount of salvage work is still effected subject to the latter principles and not under any contract.

---

[33] Such a person becomes liable as if an indorser: Bills of Exchange Act, s. 56. And it seems that, on principle, he has the rights of one too, including the right to sue the acceptor (e.g. Chalmers & Guest on *Bills of Exchange*, 14th ed. 1991, p.455).

[34] For the meaning of 'maritime' in this context, see *The Goring* [1988] 1 All E.R. 641 (non-tidal waters of the Thames not maritime).

[35] E.g. *The Troilus* [1951] A.C. 820.

The requirement of 'voluntariness' means that normally the crew of a ship cannot claim salvage from the owners[36] for saving it, though they can once the vessel has been abandoned[37] if they then return to her: on the other hand, it seems clear that the mere fact that it may be a criminal offence for the owner or master of a ship to fail to go to the assistance of another vessel in distress[38] will not affect the right to salvage[39].

Entitlement to salvage relates to property that the salvor has saved, or at least contributed to[40] the rescue of. The burden of a salvage award falls on all those who have any interest in the property saved. Moreover, 'property', it should be noted, is widely construed in the salvage context. Where ship and cargo are salved, for instance, then the salvor has a claim not only against the physical corpus of both, but also against the shipowner's claim for freight relating to that cargo: again, where a passenger ship is salved, the salvor has a claim against any unpaid passage-monies. In neither case would the monies have been earned but for the salvor's efforts.

8-14

On the other hand, it is a vital principle of salvage that the value of property saved marks the limit of any entitlement of the salvor. If he saves nothing his award is nil, however meritorious he may have been: no cure, no pay. (There is one interesting exception here: reflecting the overriding public policy against marine pollution, Lloyds Open Form provides for a limited award for anti-pollution measures even if the ultimate salvage fails[41]). Again, if what he successfully saves is of small or trifling value, so also will be his recovery.

Note the limitation to property. Saving of life at sea does not, as such, carry any reward. (It is not, however, irrelevant. If property and life are saved at the same time, the amount of any award against the property may be increased: and there is a statutory jurisdiction[42] in the Secretary of State for Transport to reward life salvors out of public funds in cases of 'pure' life salvage).

8-15

Technically, a shipowner who refuses salvage services can be made to pay for them nevertheless, at least if he acts unreasonably[43]. On the other hand, salvage services in practice are nearly always rendered by agreement between the parties, except occasionally in the case of abandoned cargo.

---

36 E.g. *The Portreath* [1923] P 155.

37 E.g. *The Albionic* [1942] P 81 (but in fact the ship had not been abandoned, so the claim failed).

38 Merchant Shipping Act 1894, s. 442; Maritime Conventions Act 1911, s. 6.

39 As, indeed, is made clear in one case by the statute concerned: Maritime Conventions Act 1911, s. 6(2).

40 E.g. *The Camellia* (1884) 9 P.D. 27.

41 The details of this are unfortunately beyond the scope of this book.

42 Merchant Shipping Act 1894, s. 544.

43 E.g. *The Kangaroo* [1918] P 327.

8-16   The amount of any salvage award is settled, in the case of Lloyds Open Form and similar standard form agreements by arbitration, and elsewhere by the court. There is no fixed formula, except that the award cannot be for more than the value of the property saved: matters in account include the value of property saved, whether the salvor was a professional salvor with vessels constantly on standby (if he was, he gets more); the amount of effort and danger to the salvor and to the salved vessel; the competence and speed of the salvage services; the availability of other salvage services, and so on.

The place of salvage in restitution law

8-17   Despite its traditional treatment in books on restitution, there is some doubt as to the precise relation between salvage and the rest of the law of restitution. True, salvage is about benefit to property owners, in that salvage awards depend on some benefit having been rendered, and are to some extent governed by the amount of any such benefit. It is also the case that the distinction drawn in English law between land and sea salvage can to some extent be justified in terms of general restitutionary principles. It is probably also true that the public policy arguments in favour of recovery for the necessitous intervener are much stronger in the case of maritime salvage. Not only is there likely to be a lack of alternative sources of assistance for a vessel in distress to call on, but life as well as property is more likely to be in serious danger: furthermore, almost universal insurance including cover for salvage charges means that it is less likely that parties will be saddled with a liability they cannot reasonably bear.

On the other hand, it is perhaps more realistic to regard salvage as *sui generis* rather than to try to integrate it too closely into the rest of the law. The connection between awards and the value of property saved (and hence benefit to the recipient of the services) is by no means direct: the element of reward given to professional salvors for keeping vessels on standby can hardly be said to reflect the benefit to any particular vessel owner. Furthermore, as has already been mentioned, a great deal of salvage is effected under standard forms of contract which provide for the amount payable to be settled by arbitration. The liabilities incurred under such a contract can hardly be called restitutionary.

CHAPTER 9

COMPULSION AND CONTRIBUTION

1 THE RIGHT TO RECOUPMENT

Suppose you owe X a debt of £1,000. If you force me to pay it for you, I have a remedy for money paid under duress[1]; it makes no difference that I paid your creditor rather then you directly. But now change the facts slightly: assume that I am forced to pay X (and hence benefit you), not by any act of yours, but by reason of some right that X has against me. For example, I may have guaranteed your debt to X: or X may have a lien over my goods in respect of it, or some statutory or other right of recourse against me or my property if you do not pay. Now, in such a case duress is clearly out of the question: nevertheless, I may well have a right to recoupment from you on other principles which are dealt with here.

The right to recoupment is generally dependent on proof by the plaintiff (1) that he discharged an obligation of the defendant[2]; (2) that he was compellable[3] to do so[4], either by action or by seizure of his property; and (3) that, as between himself and the defendant, the latter was primarily liable to pay. It is well-established in the specific cases listed below, but may well be extendable to analogous situations.

9-01

Sureties

A surety[5] called on to pay the principal debt can recoup his payment from the debtor. He can also claim to be subrogated to any security for

9-02

---

[1] On which see Chapter 4 above.

[2] So an employer cannot recover sick pay from a tortfeasor who injures his employee: to the extent that his employer continues to pay him, the employee has suffered no loss for which he can sue, and hence no liability of the wrongdoer has been discharged by the payment. See *Metropolitan Police Receiver v. Croydon Corp.* [1957] 1 All E.R. 78.

[3] He need not actually have been sued: it is enough that he paid, being liable or practically compellable (e.g. by the exercise of a lien) to do so.

[4] *Stott v. W. Yorkshire Road Car Co.* [1971] 2 Q.B. 651 (contribution between tortfeasors: plaintiff failed because he could not show he was legally compellable to pay at all). But there is now a statutory exception in this case: Civil Liability (Contribution) Act 1978, s. 1(4).

[5] Including a person who, while not legally liable for the principal debt, has charged his property to guarantee it; see e.g. *Smith v. Wood* [1929] 1 Ch. 14; *Re Marley* [1976] 1 W.L.R. 952.

the debt held by the creditor. A sub-surety has a similar restitutionary right against the surety, as well as any right he may have in contract[6].

For obvious reasons, however, this does not work the other way round. A surety can never sue a sub-surety, however much he may have saved him[7]. Traditionally, this is put on the ground that surety and sub-surety are not sureties 'in the same degree': the real reason is that, as between them, the sub-surety's liability is regarded as merely secondary, and hence any enrichment on his part is not unjustified.

Leases

9-03   A lessee who assigns his lease remains liable for rent *vis-à-vis* the lessor, notwithstanding the assignment. If called on to pay it, however, he can in turn recover from the present tenant[8]; if the landlord holds any security for the rent, it is suggested that the assignor can claim to be subrogated to it[9]. Indeed, there is no need for the lessee-claimant to be liable to be sued for the rent: it is enough if he is liable to distress in respect of it[10]. On principle it is suggested that a sub-lessee ought to have a similar right against the head lessor if forced (e.g. by distress) to pay the head rent[11], though such claims are rare[12].

9-04   However, the doctrine is limited in two ways. First, a head lessee cannot claim against an assignee's subtenant even if he has been sued for rent under the head lease and hence saved the sublease[13]. Although it may seem odd to deny a lessee out of possession reimbursement from a sub-lessee in possession, the rule can no doubt be justified by arguing that, as between them, the former is apparently regarded as primarily liable for the rent under the head-lease.

---

6   The right which is independent of contract will matter where A and B are co-sureties and C, a sub-surety of A, seeks to recover from B.

7   *Craythorne v. Swinburne* (1807) 14 Ves. 160.

8   *Moule v. Garrett* (1872) L.R. 7 Ex. 101. As against the immediate assignee the assignor has a parallel right in contract, since any assignment contains an implied covenant to indemnify the assignor. But this will obviously not work as against a subsequent assignee, who will not be in privity of contract with him.

9   *Cf Harberton (Lord) v. Bennett* (1829) Beatty 386.

10   *Whitham v. Bullock* [1939] 2 K.B. 81 (lessee divided land and assigned part to A, part to B: A held able to recover from B when landlord lawfully distrained on A for B's rent, whether or not A could in strict law be sued for it).

11   See *Eaton v. Donegal Tweed Co.* (1934) L.J.C.C.R. 81.

12   Doubtless because most sub-lessees choose to apply for relief against forfeiture under L.P.A. 1925, s. 146. But even here the question might be important, e.g. if the head rent was larger than the sub-rent, or if the sub-lease was of only part of the land subject to the head-rent.

13   *Johnson v. Wild* (1890) 44 Ch. D. 146; *Bonner v. Tottenham B.S.* [1899] 1 Q.B. 161.

Secondly, while it is not necessary that the claimant should have been liable to be sued for the rent, it appears no claim is available except against a lessee who could have been: other liabilities in the defendant, e.g. to distress, apparently do not count[14]. Hence one of several sublessees cannot recover from the other sublessee if he pays the whole of the head rent[15]. This second limitation is harder to defend: it may be, however, that the release of the defendant from a liability that was not of the latter's own making should be regarded as too remote to form the subject of an unjustified enrichment claim.

Other rights of recourse

On similar principles to those applicable to sureties and lessees, anyone who has become legally liable to pay a debt primarily owed by someone else[16] can *prima facie* recover from the main debtor once he has paid it, and claim the benefit of any security held by the creditor[17]. This category includes those, such as bonded warehouse owners, who are liable to pay excise duty on goods not owned by them but removed unlawfully from their premises[18]: sellers of partly paid shares[19]: and indorsers[20] and other transferors[21] of bills of exchange. However, any extension must be pragmatic, and must presumably not subvert other areas of the law. Property insurers, for instance, cannot as a matter of tort recover against those responsible for damaging property except by relying on subrogation or assignment[22]: nor can underwriters of personal injury insurance claim from tortfeasors[23]. It is unlikely that the courts will allow these rules to be upset by the use of unjustified enrichment.   9-05

Furthermore, an analogous right protects those who are not legally liable to pay another's debts, but who are otherwise forced by operation of law to discharge another's obligation. Thus in *Exall v. Partridge*[24], the plaintiff left a vehicle on premises leased by the defendant, whereupon the landlord lawfully distrained on it for rent: he successfully recovered the   9-06

---

[14] For possible reasons for this, see below.

[15] *Hunter v. Hunt* (1845) 1 C.B. 300 (*contra, Webber v. Smith* (1689) 2 Vern 103).

[16] Or, it is suggested, who has given security for the debt: see note above.

[17] *Duncan, Fox v. North & South Wales Bank* (1880) 6 App. Cas. 1.

[18] As in *Brook's Wharf v. Goodman* [1937] 1 K.B. 534.

[19] E.g., *Nevill's case* (1870) LR 6 Ch. App. 43.

[20] *Sleigh v. Sleigh* (1850) 5 Ex. 514: see now Bills of Exchange Act 1882, s. 55(2).

[21] *Ex. p. Bishop* (1880) 15 Ch. D. 400.

[22] *Simpson v. Thomson* (1877) 3 App. Cas. 279.

[23] Note that *Metropolitan Police Receiver v. Croydon Corp.* [1957] 2 Q.B. 154 will not help the tortfeasor here, since insurance payments are not deducted from damage awards.

[24] (1799) 8 T.R. 308.

amount he was forced to pay from the defendant. Again, if my property is wrongfully but effectively charged for someone else's debt, I have a right to recoupment from the debtor or any surety of his[25], together with a right to invoke the rules of marshalling to obtain the benefit of any other security pledged for the same debt[26]. Presumably, a similar rule applies to liens: a situation that could well arise if (for example) I buy goods in the hands of a third party over which, unknown to me, he has a lien in respect of some debt owed by a previous owner[27]. There are numerous other miscellaneous examples.

2 THE RIGHT TO CONTRIBUTION

9–07   Contribution is a sub-species of recoupment. In recoupment my claim is that I have involuntarily discharged an obligation that should have been wholly borne by you, rather than me: in contribution, it is that both of us were (as between ourselves) equally liable to bear it, but that I have paid more than my fair share.

Contribution claimants mainly (though not exclusively) fall into four categories: concurrent debtors; co-sureties; insurers; those concurrently liable for the same damage at common law (ie tortfeasors and contract-breakers), and trustees jointly liable for the same breach of trust. However, since the latter two are now covered by statute they will be dealt with together.

Concurrent debtors

9–08   Where two or more people are concurrently[28] liable for the same debt, any debtor who pays more than his fair share has a right to contribution against the others[29]. This rule applies not only to concurrent debtors as such, but also to those in analogous positions, such as partners. It is of course open to co-debtors to agree among themselves the proportions in which they bear the ultimate responsibility: if they do not, the solvent[30] debtors each pay equally.

---

25 *Ex. p. Salting* (1883) 25 Ch. D. 148

26 *Ex. p. Alston* (1868) LR 4 Ch. App. 168

27 There are a number of other possible cases where a non-owner can create a valid lien and hence trigger recovery: e.g. where the lienee is an innkeeper, or under the rule in *Tappenden v. Artus* [1964] 2 Q.B. 185.

28 I.e. jointly, or severally, or jointly and severally.

29 Except, perhaps, where the surety from whom contribution is sought became a surety purely at the request of the creditor. *Sed Quaere.*

30 It is clear in the case of co-sureties that the liabilities of insolvent sureties are disregarded for these purposes (see *Re Arcedeckne* (1883) 24 Ch. D. 709). It is suggested that concurrent debtors should be in no different position.

Co-sureties

A similar principle applies to co-sureties: one surety having paid can recover a proportion against the others[31], provided of course that he had himself become liable to pay the principal debt[32], and possibly subject to an obligation to exhaust first any practical remedy he may have against the principal debtor. *Prima facie* individual sureties, like concurrent debtors, pay equally in the absence of agreement between them. But this is displaced where the liability of one or more sureties is limited, and the maximum sums concerned are different. Here, it seems, liability is apportioned proportionately to the respective maximum limits[33] (save that, if any surety's liability is unlimited, his maximum is reckoned as the amount of the debt[34]).

9-09

Insurers

Where the same loss is insured by more than one insurer, an insurer who pays the whole loss can recover against any other insurer liable[35] in respect of it. At common law it seems that the insurers must have insured not only the same loss but the same risk. Thus in *North British & Mercantile Insurance Co. v. London, Liverpool & Globe Insurance Co.*[36] it was held that where bailees and bailors both insured goods, the bailees' insurer could not claim contribution from the bailors' underwriter; the insurances may have been on the same goods, but they were not on the same interests in those goods. But this principle may not have survived the enactment of the Civil Liability (Contribution) Act 1978[37].

9-10

There is some doubt about the position where the insurer who pays has a clause in the policy limiting his liability to a rateable proportion in the case of double insurance. Having paid the whole claim, can he then claim contribution against the other insurer? At common law it was held that he could not: the excess over and above his own rateable proportion was regarded as a voluntary payment and hence irrecoverable, whether or

---

[31] Including those whose property is charged but who are not personally liable: *Smith v. Wood* [1929] 1 Ch. 14.

[32] On what this entails, see *Hay v. Carter* [1935] Ch. 397.

[33] *Ellesmere Brewery v. Cooper* [1896] 1 Q.B. 75.

[34] See *Naumann v. Northcote* (unreported, C.A., 7 February 1978).

[35] Including an insurer who was once liable, but has ceased to be because of failure to give due notice of a claim: *Legal & General Assurance v. Drake Assurance* [1992] 1 All E.R. 283.

[36] (1876) 5 Ch. D. 569.

[37] Section 1 of which enacts a general right to contribution as between those liable in respect of the same damage, whether in contract, tort or otherwise. Bailees' and bailors' insurers seem to come within this criterion, especially since it now seems that the liability of an insurer to pay out on a loss is a liability in damages and not in debt (see Hirst J's decision in *The Italia Express* [1992] 2 Lloyds Rep. 281).

not at the time he knew of the existence of the other insurer[38]. However, it is arguable that the position has now been reversed by the Civil Liability (Contribution) Act 1978. Section 1(4) of this Act provides that contribution is available between two or more parties in respect of any damage wherever the person claiming it has settled the claim against him in good faith, whether or not he was in fact liable. Assuming that an insurer is a person 'liable in respect of any damage' within s 1(1) of the Act[39], it is difficult to avoid the conclusion that a 'rateable proportion' clause in the plaintiff's policy will any longer protect the defendant.

The distribution of the loss in the case of differing limits on liability is also a matter of controversy. As between liability insurers it is on the basis of the amount each insurer would have had to pay under the claim had he been solely liable[40]; with property insurers, it is probably the same as in the case of sureties (ie the proportion between the maximum liabilities under the policies)[41].

Concurrent wrongdoers and trustees

9-11   This subject is covered very adequately in works on tort and trusts[42], and for that reason will be dealt with relatively briefly.

The basis for contribution between wrongdoers is now entirely statutory. At common law no such right existed in the case of tortfeasors or contract-breakers; there were pre-existing equitable rules for contribution between trustees, but these were limited to a rigid basis of equal division of the loss[43].

Section 1 of the Civil Liability (Contribution) Act 1978 now provides for a general right of contribution between anyone liable for the same loss, whatever the basis of liability. The measure of contribution is fixed at whatever sum the court considers just and equitable (s.2(1)); but this sum must be fixed as between those parties before the court, with no account being taken of anyone else's possible liability[44].

A limited exception is introduced by the statute to the normal rule in contribution and recoupment cases, that reimbursement is only available to a claimant who was compellable to discharge the liability concerned. Largely for reasons of convenience, s.1(4) provides that a defendant who

---

[38] *Legal & General Assurance v. Drake Insurance* [1992] 1 All E.R. 283.

[39] On which see *The Italia Express*, note 37 above.

[40] *Commercial Union v. Hayden* [1977] 1 All E.R. 441.

[41] Assumed, but not decided, in *Commercial Union v. Hayden*, above.

[42] E.g. *Clerk & Lindsell on Torts*, 16th ed., §2-57; *Snell's Equity*, 29th ed., 296 ff.

[43] The old rule in *Bahin v. Hughes* (1886) 31 Ch. D. 390.

[44] *Mayfield v. Llewellyn* [1961] 1 W.L.R. 119. This is admittedly a rough and ready way of dealing with the question of enrichment: but it is probably justified on practical grounds.

has *bona fide* settled a claim against him can claim contribution whether or not he was in fact liable to pay[45].

Other cases

The four categories above are not exhaustive, but reflect a more general rule that where several people are commonly subject to some obligation, any one of them who bears more than his fair share of it is entitled to reimbursement from the others. Other examples include partners[46], and company directors jointly liable for misfeasance[47].   **9-12**

3 POSSIBLE EXTENSIONS OF RECOUPMENT AND CONTRIBUTION

Recoupment and contribution proper concern forced discharge of obligations. What they have in common is (a) a debt or other obligation affecting the defendant; (b) which the plaintiff has been compelled to discharge; and (c) which, as between plaintiff and defendant, ought wholly or partly to have been discharged by the latter[48]. Logically, however, it can be argued that there is no need to limit it to these instances: the principle behind it should be extended to any case where A has been effectively forced to confer any benefit whatever on B.   **9-13**

In at least one case this logic, or something like it, is applied: this is the doctrine of general average (dealt with below). It is an open question similar thinking can be applied by analogy to cover other benefits, in particular in the case of emergency action taken for the defendant's benefit which incidentally affects others' interests. Suppose, for instance, that, in the course of putting out a fire in my house, firemen enter on your land and do substantial damage to it. You clearly cannot sue the fire authority, since they had a right to act as they did[49]: on the other hand, you have been forced to suffer considerable prejudice for my benefit, and there is much to be said for allowing you a measure of restitutionary recovery in respect of this. Again, imagine two ships owned by A and B moored together in an exposed position. A storm blows up; fearing for their safety,

---

[45] Section 1(4). The previous rule was different: *Stott v. West Yorkshire Road Car Co.* [1971] 2 Q.B. 651.

[46] E.g. *Re Royal Bank of Australia* (1856) 6 D, M & G 572.

[47] E.g. *Ramskill v. Edwards* (1885) 31 Ch. D. 100.

[48] Or, put another way, that the defendant's enrichment is unjustified. This also explains why the surety cannot claim against the sub-surety: there is nothing unjust about the latter taking the benefit of the former's payment.

[49] The fire services understandably have extensive powers of entry on, and interference with, property in the course of their operations: e.g. Fire Services Act 1947, s. 30.

the crew of A's ship cast off the mooring lines and stand out to sea; B's ship thereupon goes adrift and is damaged. The emergency precludes any liability of A to B in tort: on the other hand, it seems hard that B should bear the entire loss of saving A's property. At this stage it must remain an open question whether the law of restitution may come to the rescue[50].

4   GENERAL RULES CONCERNING RECOUPMENT AND CONTRIBUTION

Independent nature of the right

9-14   Although the right to recoupment or contribution obviously depends on the existence of a valid obligation owed by the defendant to the original claimant (since otherwise the defendant would not be enriched at all), it is an independent right. It is therefore unaffected by any personal defence which may have become available to the defendant vis-à-vis the original claimant after[51] the cause of action arose[52]. In particular, claims for contribution and recoupment can be brought despite any defence of limitation[53] or compromise[54] that would have applied had the original claimant proceeded directly against the defendant.

Voluntary subjection and the problem of officiousness[55]

9-15   If I voluntarily satisfy your obligation to X, no question of recoupment arises: an essential element of the cause of action, compulsion, is missing[56]. But what if I voluntarily guarantee your debt

---

[50]   True, in the case of leases it seems necessary that the plaintiff has discharged a legally enforceable liability for rent: see note 15 above. But it is suggested that there is no reason why this should be a general requirement.

[51]   But obviously not before: if the person from whom contribution is sought would have had a good defence to any claim at the time the original claim arose, he has not been enriched at all.

[52]   *Legal & General Assurance v. Drake Insurance* [1992] 1 All E.R. 283 (contribution between insurers available despite lapse of claim against second underwriter due to lack of timely notice).

[53]   Section 1(3) of the 1978 Act makes this clear in the case of statutory contribution, but this merely replicates the common law and equitable rules anyway; see e.g. *Wolmershausen v. Gullick* [1893] 2 Q.B. 514.

[54]   See *Logan v. Uttlesford D.C.* (1986) 136 New L.J. 541 (statutory contribution). Note, though, that a *release* of one joint wrongdoer or contractor releases the others: if subsequently one of the others pays, his claim for contribution can be met by a defence that he was not liable to pay in the first place.

[55]   See Chapter 14 below for a general discussion of the problems of officiousness.

[56]   E.g. *Legal & General Assurance v. Drake Insurance* [1992] 1 All E.R. 283. Of course, if you have a chance to reject my interference but choose to accept it instead, I may have a claim against you on the basis of free acceptance: but that is different.

without your approval and I am then duly compelled to pay it? In *Owen v. Tate*[57] the Court of Appeal denied such a voluntary guarantor recourse against the principal debtor on the basis that he had acted officiously.

With respect, however, it must be doubtful whether there is any need for such a separate doctrine in cases of recoupment. First, it was not necessary to the decision in *Owen v. Tate*: the case could equally well have been decided on the sounder basis that in the circumstances there had been no free acceptance of the benefit of the payment. Secondly, in any case it is subject to severe limitations. It seems to have no place in contribution between co-sureties: any co-surety can claim contribution, whatever the relation (or lack of it) between him and the other sureties[58]. Equally, it does not apply in at least some cases of recoupment[59].

5   A SPECIAL CASE - GENERAL AVERAGE

Suppose a cargo-carrying vessel gets into difficulties. In order to complete the voyage, extraordinary expenses are incurred for (eg) towage or repairs; or - more drastically - some of the cargo has to be jettisoned or discharged. In such a case the shipowner or cargo owner, as the case may be, has a claim against the other participants in the adventure for rateable contribution to the loss according to the benefit received by the latter. Although as between ship and cargo this is largely regulated by contract[60], the right is a general one and equally applies as between cargo owners who are not in privity of contract. The expenses must be extraordinary[61] and reasonable, and incurred in order to avert an actual danger[62] to the whole adventure; rather oddly, they must also be forced on the participants by force of circumstances, and not by (eg) government action[63]. Reflecting the principle that restitutionary rights are subject to any contrary agreement between the parties, no claim lies by the shipowner in respect of loss or expenditure arising from a cause for which he is responsible under the contract of carriage[64].

9-16

---

[57] [1975] 2 All E.R. 129.

[58] Rowlatt, *Principal & Surety*, 4th ed., pp.152-153.

[59] E.g. accommodation bills: Bills of Exchange Act 1882, s. 59(3).

[60] Virtually all contracts for carriage of goods by sea provide for adjustment of general average according to extra-statutory provisions known as the York-Antwerp Rules.

[61] E.g. *Société Nouvelle v. Spillers* [1917] 1 K.B. 865.

[62] *Watson v Fireman's Fund* [1922] 2 K.B. 355

[63] *Athel Line v. London, etc., Insurance* (1945) 78 Lloyds Rep. 414.

[64] *Strang Steel v. Scott* (1889) 14 App. Cas. 601. See in particular the Hague-Visby Rules appended to the Carriage of Goods by Sea Act 1971, r.4(2).

CHAPTER 10

BENEFITS CONFERRED THROUGH THIRD PARTIES: 'TRACING'

Most of this book deals with claims for reimbursement for benefits received at the hands of the plaintiff. I pay you money by mistake; I paint your house at your request, and so on; in all these cases the person providing the benefit and the person seeking restitution are one and the same. In this chapter, by contrast, the defendant's enrichment comes through the intervention of a third party. Typically, we are talking about unravelling the consequences of fraud: the third party being the villain, the claimant his victim and the defendant a person who receives or handles the fruits of his peculation later on. But dishonesty is not *de rigueur*: trustees, executors and banks equally can and do make mistakes that divert to me assets that should have gone to you, and hence raise questions of how the resulting imbalance should be corrected.

Before we start, however, a terminological point. Taken at its widest, this chapter could swallow up the whole of the law of property. Suppose your car is stolen and I buy it; or suppose your trustee makes a present to me of shares belonging to the trust. If I still have the car (or the shares) you have a good claim against me to get them back. But it is not a *restitutionary* claim; it is simply to be given back what remained yours all along, whether at law or in equity[1]. We will not be dealing with it here; instead, we will concentrate on cases of unjust enrichment proper, as where (for instance) I have sold the car or the shares before you approach me, and you then look to me to reimburse to you the amount I got for them. Third party enrichments fall naturally into two categories: first, assets transferred from you to me by some other person, and secondly assets which ought to have gone to you but have found their way into my hands.

1   ASSETS TRANSFERRED

Receipt of money representing plaintiff's assets – common law

We start with an abstract proposition. If a third party without lawful **10-02** excuse causes a payment to be made to me which derives from money or assets belonging to you, you can *prima facie* sue me for money had and

---

[1]   *Cf* the discussion at para. 1-25 above.

received. Assume your butler steals your cheque-book, forges your signature on a cheque and gives it to me; I then cash it. Or your agent, whom you authorise to transfer funds on your behalf in the course of your business, fraudulently transfers money to me in order to pay a debt of his in circumstances where I am not a bona fide purchaser. Or again, a bank computer error causes £1,000 to be debited to your account and credited to mine. In all three cases you can sue me for the amount I received[2]: to that extent[3] I am unjustifiably enriched at your expense. It does not matter whether your property from which mine arose was in the form of money, or a bank balance, or some other thing: if X steals your car, sells it and immediately hands the price to me, I must still account to you. Nor does it matter that I was not the direct recipient: it would make no difference to the first example above if the cheque had been made out to a friend of mine who had cashed it and immediately given the proceeds to me[4].

A number of points now fall to be made about this action, which lies on principle for the full amount received, and is independent of whether the recipient was in good faith.

Benefit 'from the plaintiff's money': identifying the source of the benefit

10-03   The full name of the action for money had and received is money had and received *to the use of the plaintiff*, in other words, to establish the cause of action, you must show that my gain derives from your money. This in turn breaks down into two separate requirements.

The first necessity is that the ultimate source of my gain must have been something you had title to at common law but have since been deprived of: this is, after all, a common law cause of action. So a stolen car will do, as will money in my bank account: on the other hand, an interest under a bare trust will not.

Secondly, and more importantly, you must be able to identify the money received by me with that property, that is to link your loss to my gain. What sort of tie does this entail? On the authorities, it must be one satisfying three criteria: (a) you must have been wrongfully deprived of

---

2   Forgery: *Banque Belge v. Hambrouck* [1921] 1 K.B. 321 (as interpreted in *Agip (Africa) v. Jackson* (1990) [1992] 4 All E.R. 451). Fraud: *Lipkin Gorman v. Karpnale* [1992] 4 All E.R. 512. The author knows of no case concerning bank error.

3   Subject to change of position; see below and also Chapter 15.

4   *Banque Belge v. Hambrouck* [1921] 1 K.B. 321 suggests this, in so far as it held Mlle Spanoghe liable to the plaintiffs. Mlle Spanoghe was an indirect, not a direct, recipient. True, Millett J suggested in *Agip (Africa) v. Jackson* [1992] 4 All E.R. 385, 400-401 that the indirect recipient only incurred liability while he still had the money. But it is difficult to see why; he is adequately protected by the defence of change of position as it is.

your proprietary right; (b) the money I received must have been derived from it, directly or indirectly, by means of one or more sales or exchanges; and (c) the process of exchange must not have involved mixing at any intermediate stage.

To demonstrate point (a), assume you pay X £100 cash as prepayment for goods, whereupon X gives the very same notes to me; X then fails to deliver the goods. You have a right against X, but not against me: you have not been deprived of any proprietary interest with which the notes I received can be identified[5]. Points (b) and (c) are neatly illustrated by *Agip (Africa) v. Jackson*[6]. As a result of the activities of a rogue named Zdiri, Agip's bank in Tunisia debited Agip's account by $526,000 and asked Lloyds Bank in London to credit Baker (a company controlled by Zdiri) with the same sum. Lloyds Bank did so, being put in funds at a later stage by Agip's bank. Baker then transferred the money to Jackson. Agip's action against Jackson for money had and received failed. Since Lloyds had credited Baker before being paid by Agip's bank, the monies received by Baker and Jackson were not genuine exchange products of Agip's funds (see (b)). And furthermore, Agip's bank could not have transferred the requisite sums to Lloyds without mixing them with other funds in the New York clearing system, thus preventing requirement (c) from being fulfilled.

10-04

A personal or proprietary claim? The misuse of the word 'tracing'

At first sight the head of money had and received just outlined looks like a simple property claim: the plaintiff pointing to a sum of money in the hands of the defendant and saying 'That is mine.' For this reason, and also because the plaintiff cannot even get his action off the ground unless he can show some original legal proprietary interest infringed, it is often referred to as 'common law tracing'.

10-05

But this is misconceived. The requirement of an original proprietary interest simply means that in its absence there is nothing unjust about the defendant's enrichment. It says nothing about the nature of the action, which is one for a money judgment, and based on receipt, not retention at the time of the claim. Indeed, the action lies (subject to the defence of change of position, below) even though there is nothing remaining in the defendant's hands representing what the plaintiff originally lost.

This leaves one problematical point. Suppose I cash a cheque forged by your butler in my favour: before I have spent the cash, I go bankrupt.

10-06

[5] Compare *Eldan Services v. Chandag Motors* [1990] 3 All E.R. 459; a person who pays for something in advance is not wrongfully deprived of his money even if he does not get what he paid for.
[6] [1992] 4 All E.R. 451.

If the above argument is right, one might have thought you had to take your place with my other general creditors; yet in fact, you can get back your money in full from my trustee in bankruptcy. How so? The answer lies, not in any proprietary basis of the action, but in its receipt-based nature. It is not that assets representing your original property themselves belong to you; rather, they are – so to speak – impressed with a stamp, such that no-one can receive them (other than by way of bona fide purchase, etc.) without coming under a duty to account *in personam* to you[7]. And this includes my trustee in bankruptcy; as and when he takes the cash from me as forming part of my assets, he is himself treated as a receiver of it and hence comes under a separate personal liability to account.

Defences

Bona fide purchase

10-07   It is sometimes said that bona fide purchase is no bar to common law tracing. This is simply not true. If the recipient, or any predecessor in title of his, has given value in exchange for money alleged to represent the claimant's assets, he is protected from liability[8]. Moreover, this protection is complete, and does not simply extend to the extent of the value given, as he would be in the case of change of position.

Value for these purposes means consideration under a valid contract: a void transaction such as a gaming contract will not do. Presumably the same goes for a contract binding in honour only[9].

Change of position

10-08   In so far as the recipient has innocently incurred expenditure or obligations in the faith that he can keep what he has got, he is protected under this head. *Lipkin Gorman v. Karpnale*[10], besides establishing the

---

7   "Liability depends upon receipt by the defendant of the plaintiff's money..." – *Agip (Africa) v. Jackson* [1992] 4 All E.R. 451, 463 (Fox LJ).

8   E.g. *Lipkin Gorman v. Karpnale* [1992] 4 All E.R. 409 (C.A.). In fact the House of Lords held that the defendant was not a bona fide purchaser (see [1992] 4 All E.R. 512); but that does not affect the point in the text.

9   *Lipkin Gorman v. Karpnale* [1992] 4 All E.R. 512 (receipt in payment of gambling debts does not count as bona fide purchase). *Quaere* how far this goes, however. If a solicitor pays counsel with stolen money, must counsel (who cannot sue for his fees) refund in full to the victim of the theft?

10   [1992] 4 All E.R. 512.

general availability of this defence[11], illustrates the process neatly. A partner in a firm of solicitors gambled the firm's money at the Playboy Club: the club, who did not count as bona fide purchasers, had to repay the amount staked, but were unable to deduct the partner's own winnings. Similarly in *Agip (Africa) v. Jackson*[12] the defendants, Manx accountants, had credited to accounts controlled by them assets derived from monies filched from Agip, but had then innocently accounted for them to their principals, who were in fact party to the fraud. Millett J held that even if the defendants were liable (which in the event they were not) their innocent change of position would have protected them in any case.

Receipt of goods representing plaintiff's assets: common law

In the ordinary case where A's goods are transferred to B by the machinations of a third party C, there is (unlike the case of money payments) no need for restitution: A merely sues B in tort for conversion[13], with no questions asked as to whether B was innocent or otherwise, or indeed whether he still has the goods. But this will not always work: in particular, it breaks down where the goods received by B (i) are not the original ones owned by A but their proceeds; or (ii) *a fortiori*, are proceeds not of goods but something else, such as money, in A's hands.

10-09

One thing is clear: whatever claim A does have against the proceeds of his property in B's hands, he is not without more to be taken as their owner. If a thief steals my Ford and exchanges it for a Rover I may have some sort of claim to the Rover, but I am not the owner of it. If I were, I could sue anyone who bought it from the thief, however innocently, in conversion; but it is clear I cannot do this. So, for example, in *Commercial Banking Co. of Sydney v. Mann*[14], Mann's partner stole cheques from the partnership and then changed them for banker's drafts which he cashed at the defendant bank. An action by the partners against the bank for conversion failed: true, the drafts in the bank's hands derived from their property, but this did not make them the owners of them so as to allow them to bring conversion in respect of them.

---

[11] On which see Chapter 15 below.

[12] [1992] 4 All E.R. 385. In the event this point did not fall for decision by the Court of Appeal (see [1992] 4 All E.R. 451).

[13] Though it might just be argued that conversion, though nominally a tort, ought really to be regarded as a restitutionary cause of action. The measure of recovery, after all, is the value of what is converted, not the loss suffered by the plaintiff. Professor Birks, indeed, comes close to arguing this in *Commercial Aspects of Trusts and Fiduciary Obligations*, ed. McKendrick, Chapter 8, at pp.159-160.

[14] [1961] A.C. 1.

10-10   Nevertheless, there are two situations where a common law claim will lie against the possessor of property which is the proceeds of something belonging to the plaintiff.

The first arises where the possessor sells those proceeds. Here, there is no reason in logic not to treat him in the same way as any other receiver of money representing other people's property, i.e. as liable to a claim in money had and received[15]. The fact that he, rather than somebody else, turned them into money ought to be irrelevant.

Secondly, where a *mala fide* recipient takes my property and sells or exchanges it, I am (it seems) entitled *as against him*, though not against anyone else, to adopt the exchange and regard its product as mine. This is the best explanation of *Taylor v. Plumer*[16], a decision dealt with elsewhere, under restitution for wrongs[17].

Receipt of money or goods representing plaintiff's assets: equity

10-11   The common law rights mentioned above presuppose an initial proprietary right recognised at common law. The claimant who starts out with an equitable claim[18] to assets has superficially analogous, but in fact rather different, claims against recipients of those assets or their proceeds. These claims are of two types[19].

First, in certain cases the recipient is liable personally to repay the value of what he has received, in rather the same way that the recipient of goods may be liable in conversion for their value.

10-12   Secondly, where the property subject to the original equitable right has been exchanged or turned into something else, the owner can claim a substitutive equitable right in its product by the process known as 'tracing'.

Equitable personal claims

Suppose, in the winding-up of an estate, that assets are misdirected by the personal representatives to those not entitled. The leading case is *Ministry of Health v. Simpson*[20]. Where executors distributed assets

---

15   Why was this claim not advanced in respect of the proceeds of the banker's draft in *Lipkin Gorman v. Karpnale* [1992] 4 All E.R. 512? Presumably because the Playboy Club had spent them and thus could plead change of position.

16   (1815) 3 M & S 562.

17   See para. 11-11, below.

18   As for what amounts to an equitable claim for these purposes, see below.

19   Leaving aside the claim against the recipient who still has trust property and who cannot claim the protection afforded the bona fide purchaser.

20   [1951] A.C. 251.

according to a clause in a will which turned out to be invalid, the House of Lords confirmed that the recipients were liable to the next-of-kin for the value of what they had got. This was a drastic liability, independent of fault in anyone and (apparently) unaffected by any change of position on the part of the recipient. Its only palliation was that any recovery fell to be reduced by the amount that was, or could reasonably have been, recovered from the personal representatives.

It is not clear how far the principle in *Ministry of Health v. Simpson*[21] **10-13** can be generalised outside the administration of estates. In *Re Leslie Engineers*[22] Slade J was prepared to extend it to distributions in insolvency – rightly, no doubt, since there is a good deal in common between the processes of distributing the assets of the dead and the delinquent. But the real question is whether it is likely to be applied to misapplication of trust assets generally. It is suggested that the answer is no, for two reasons.

First, the rules of liability are anomalous. The lack of any defence of change of position, assuming this feature of the liability still survives[23], is indefensible. Moreover, if the basis of liability is unjustified enrichment, it is odd to give the recipient credit for what ought to have been recovered from the personal representatives: the recipient's enrichment does not become any less unjustified merely because the claimant could have been recouped from another source.

Secondly, any extension to trusts generally of a personal liability to account independent of fault would subvert the present rather carefully worked-out relation between claims to recover one's own beneficial property and claims for 'knowing receipt'[24]. Under this scheme, the wrongful recipient who still has trust assets has to give them back (property): but once he has sold or disposed of them, he is not liable to the beneficiary at all unless before he did so he knew (or perhaps ought to have known) that he was not entitled to them[25]. To superimpose on this a further head of liability based on receipt alone would clearly destroy this whole arrangement.

Equitable 'tracing' claims

Unlike so-called common law tracing, equitable tracing gives rise to **10-14** something close to what can be called (for want of anything better) a

---

21 [1951] A.C. 251.

22 [1976] 2 All E.R. 85.

23 Which is unclear since *Lipkin Gorman v. Karpnale* [1992] 4 All E.R. 512 established the general availability of this defence in restitutionary claims.

24 See generally Snell's *Equity*, 29th ed., p.193 ff.

25 It is not proposed to go into the question what degree of knowledge must be shown. Suffice it to say that *some* degree of knowledge, whether actual or constructive, is necessary: it is universally accepted that liability is not strict.

'substitutionary proprietary claim' – that is, a claim by the 'victim' to be the beneficial owner not only of original trust property but of any exchange product of it, and for that reason to be able to follow that product into the hands of anyone other than a bona fide purchaser for value. It is therefore very different from the 'receipt-based' action for money had and received.

The proprietary nature of this claim, however, cuts both ways. In particular it applies – unlike that for money had and received – only to the defendant who still has property representing the claimant's. I cannot claim my property from you if you have not still got it[26]: all I can do is claim money in substitution, which in equity I can do only if I can show that you acted with the requisite degree of knowledge to make you guilty of knowing receipt.

To establish my right to trace assets in your hands, I have to show two things: (1) that I had a sufficient equitable proprietary base to start with; and (2) that there is a sufficient connection between the asset in your hands and my original property to say that one represents the other.

(1) The equitable proprietary base

10-15
An interest as cestui que trust is the obvious, but by no means the only, basis for a tracing claim in equity. A resulting trust will do just as well, as will a situation such as that occurring in *Chase Manhattan Bank v. Israel-British Bank*[27], where assets are transferred by mistake such that equitable title remains in the transferor. So also with an interest in a deceased person's estate[28], even though this technically does not comport an equitable interest in anything in particular[29]. Indeed, the acceptable interests go even further. Although legal ownership of property pure and simple will not suffice[30], legal ownership of assets in the hands of, or under the control of, my bailee, agent, employee or other fiduciary will. Since most sizeable thefts are in practice committed by agents, employees, and the like, it follows that the victim of theft or fraud will as often as not be able to use both money had and received at common law (relying on his legal ownership) and tracing in equity (relying on his fiduciary relationship with the thief), according to which is more advantageous[31]

---

26   The tracing claim in equity gives rise to a proprietary remedy "*which depends on the continued existence of the trust property in the hands of the defendant*" – *Agip (Africa) v. Jackson* [1992] 4 All E.R. 385, 402 (Millett J). (Italics supplied).

27   [1979] 3 All E.R. 1025.

28   *Re Diplock* [1948] Ch. 465.

29   See e.g. *Comm'rs of Stamp Duties v. Livingston* [1965] A.C. 694, 707.

30   A proposition accepted in *Re Diplock*, above.

31   So, to take just one example, in *Banque Belge v. Hambrouck* [1921] 1 K.B. 321, the plaintiffs relied on both money had and received and equitable tracing.

(2) Sufficient connection

Save in one respect, the connection required is largely the same as for common law claims – i.e. that the assets in the defendant's hands represent the direct or indirect exchange product of the plaintiff's property. The exception, however, is vital and concerns mixture with other assets. We have seen that this will bar identification at common law and hence any claim for money had and received against a subsequent recipient. It will not, however, affect the process of identification in equity. Thus in *Agip (Africa) v. Jackson*[32], dealt with above, the fact that Agip's money had been mixed in the New York clearing system, while it barred any common law right, did not prevent equitable tracing (though in fact this was impossible for another reason, namely that the defendants were no longer in possession of any assets repreenting the plaintiffs' property).

10-16

This in turn, however, raises a further awkward question. Suppose various assets, including mine, are paid by you into your bank account at various times: you then buy a picture, a car, a holiday and so on, out of that account. Do I have an interest in the picture or the car? The common law ducks this issue by barring all claims at the point of mixture. Equity, by contrast, cannot do this; having decided to take mixture in its stride, it has then in the nature of things to construct some rule as to which payment in corresponds to which payment out. An arbitrary rule, of course; given that a bank account is merely an amorphous running balance between banker and customer, swelled by credits and depleted by drawings, the question as to which of the former correspond to which of the latter is not susceptible to any logical or rational answer.

10-17

With current accounts, the principle that has developed is that *prima facie* drawings are deemed to take place in the same order as credits[33], and that this applies to claims by the original equitable owners to the proceeds of those drawings[34]. Put more simply, 'first in, first out'. It follows that where my money is paid into a bank account and then that account is drawn on to provide an asset in your hands, I have a claim to that asset if, and only if[35] I can show, on the 'first in, first out' basis, that my money went into that asset[36]. If on this basis an asset was bought partly with my money and partly with yours, I have a proportionate interest in it, including any rise in its value[37].

---

32 [1992] 4 All E.R. 451.
33 *Clayton's case* (1816) 1 Mer. 572.
34 *Pennell v. Deffell* (1853) 4 D M & G 372.
35 *Hancock v. Smith* (1889) 41 Ch. D. 456; *Re Tilley's W.T.* [1967] Ch. 1179.
36 *Re Diplock* [1948] Ch. 465.
37 *Scott v. Scott* (1962) 109 C.L.R. 649.

On the other hand, the 'first in, first out' rule is heavily qualified. It does not apply to anything other than a running account[38], or where the beneficial owners of money intend 'their' funds to be mixed generally with others' monies, as where they give to a deserving cause[39], or pay in to a general investment scheme hoping for substantial returns[40]. Here, the monies in the account at the time of any claim are deemed to be derived *pari passu* from the funds of those who paid in. And *Clayton's Case* is subject to the 'wrongdoers' lien' provision below. There are *dicta*[41], but only *dicta,* that the courts retain a general discretion to disapply it in the interests of justice.

(3) A special rule: the wrongdoer's lien

10-18   The equitable tracing claim, as a substitutionary proprietary claim, is available against a wrongdoer mixing trust property with his own, just as it is against anyone else. You credit £1,000 of my trust money to your account which already contains £500, and then buy shares for £1,500 that double in value. I can claim two-thirds of those shares in respect of my £1,000 (and hence a windfall profit of £1,000)[42]. But, as mentioned above, this only works if the necessary nexus can be shown to identify the trust property with what was bought; if you had bought only £500 worth of shares and dissipated the other £1,000 I would be left high and dry. For this reason, if you are a wrongdoer, I have a further, independent right to claim a lien against all monies remaining in your account, and against anything bought with monies from it while it is still in your hands. This is significant for two reasons. First, you may be insolvent and, because of the vagaries of *Clayton's Case*[43], I may not be able positively to identify my trust property with anything you still have[44]. Secondly, even if I can get over the problem of identification, the exchange product of my property may have gone down in value. You use £1,000 of my trust fund to buy shares now worth £750. I can claim the shares as the product of my £1,000, but if I do I 'use up' £1,000 of my claim: if, on the other hand, I claim a lien over them, I only 'use up' £750 and can seek to recover the other £250 elsewhere. On the other hand, the lien only applies up to the amount of my monies that went into the account: windfall profits over and above that sum cannot be claimed[45].

---

38 *The Mecca* [1897] A.C. 286.

39 *Re British Red Cross Balkan Fund* [1914] 2 Ch. 419.

40 *Barlow Clowes International v. Vaughan* [1992] 4 All E.R. 22.

41 See *Barlow Clowes International v. Vaughan* [1992] 4 All E.R. 22, 39 (Woolf LJ).

42 *Scott v. Scott* (1962) 109 C.L.R. 649.

43 (1816) 1 Mer. 572.

44 As happened in *Re Hallett's Estate* (1880) 13 Ch. D. 696.

45 *Re Oatway* [1903] 2 Ch. 356; *Re Tilley's W.T.* [1967] Ch. 1179.

2 GAINS DIVERTED

So far we have dealt with diversion of assets – i.e. gains coming to you because some third party has caused me to be deprived of an asset whose proceeds have ended up in your hands. But there is no necessary reason why my entitlement need be based on property: there are other cases too where the law provides that accretions to your wealth represent diverted gains that really ought to have come to me, and hence that you must account for them to me. It is to these we now turn.

10-19

Profits of property or office

If I take something of yours and hire it out for my own profit, there is no difficulty in your suing me for that profit through the mechanism of waiver of tort[46]. But what if, owing to some confusion, I receive the rent of your land without actually displacing you? Even in the absence of a wrongful act, I am liable to account to you for the rent wrongfully received[47].

A similar rule applies to offices. The distinction between paid office and private investment has at times been blurred in the common law; there developed early a rule that if you received the profits of a position or office to which I am entitled, I could, as with my property, sue you for money had and received[48]. You might not have received the proceeds of an actual thing of mine, but you had done something which the law regarded as equivalent. Later this rule was extended to any payment made to someone who, however innocently, usurped the function that should have been served by the plaintiff[49].

Other cases

More commonly, however, the factor justifying restitution arises out of some relation between the parties. The simplest situation is where you receive £100 from X as my agent, or simply on my account; in either case, I can sue you in money had and received for the £100[50].

10-20

And similar principles apply in equity. Assume a trustee, without committing a breach of fiduciary duty or using trust property, receives a

---

[46] See below, para 11-08 ff.
[47] An early case is *Tottenham v. Bedingfield* (1572) Owen 35.
[48] *Arris v. Stukeley* (1677) 2 Mod. 260.
[49] *Jacob v. Allen* (1703) Salk 27 (payment to administrator; will later found; claim by executor).
[50] *Beckingham & Lambert v. Vaughan* (1616) 1 Rolle Rep. 391.

sum of money deriving from, or attributable to, his trusteeship: for instance, by being appointed a director of a company in which the trust has a shareholding and being paid as such[51]. Or assume a partner receives a sum of money that, properly construed, represents partnership profits or the price of a partnership asset. In either case it is a necessary incident of the relationship – trusteeship, partnership, etc. – that the sum concerned not be regarded as one's own but paid over or shared, as the case may be. It is this obligation which equity duly enforces by imposing a duty on the receiver to pay over what he has received to the beneficiary.

---

[51]   *Re Macadam* [1946] Ch. 73.

CHAPTER 11

RESTITUTION FOR WRONGS

In this chapter there is a shift of focus. From dealing with benefits that **11-01** reach the defendant through the act of the claimant himself, or by some third party, or by diversion of assets or profits, we now turn to the third logical possibility: benefits accruing to the defendant as a direct result of some wrong committed by him.

Three preliminary points are in order.

First, 'wrong' in this connection is used in as general a sense as **11-02** possible. It covers not only torts, but also breaches of contract, trust and fiduciary duty, all of which give rise to duties of compensation (whether we call such compensation 'damages' or not). It also extends to intellectual property infringements, whether extra-statutory such as passing-off and breach of confidence, or statutory such as patent, copyright and trade mark infringement. This is not, of course, to say that there is any all-embracing rule covering restitutionary recovery for all these varieties of wrong: only that the issues raised are similar, and they are worth dealing with together.

Secondly, this chapter deals with wrongs as a ground for, rather than merely a background to, restitution: cases, in other words, where the fact that the defendant has gained from a wrong is regarded, *without more*, as sufficient to give the plaintiff a right to restitution. An example can make this clearer. Suppose you induce me to give you £1,000 by a negligent misrepresentation. It is clear that I can recover the £1,000 in a restitutionary action: furthermore, if there is a suitable special relationship between us[1], it is equally clear that you are liable to me in tort. Nevertheless, this is not a case of restitution for wrongs; my right to £1,000 from you is based on my mistake, not your tort. Now imagine, by contrast, that you are my trustee and make £1,000 from information obtained as such. In so far as you are bound to make restitution[2], this is genuine restitution for wrongs: your duty to give me the £1,000 is genuinely based on the fact that you committed a wrong - in this case, a breach of trust.

---

[1] Under *Hedley Byrne v. Heller* [1964] A.C. 462.
[2] See below, para. 11-16 ff.

Thirdly, we are dealing here with cases where remedies are *in fact* given to reverse enrichment resulting from a wrong, whatever labels the courts attach to them. As we shall see, damages can be an unjustified enrichment remedy just as much as more traditional restitutionary remedies such as waiver of tort or account of profits; the analytical point that damages ought to reflect claimant's loss rather than defendant's gain is not necessarily borne out in practice.

11-03   All this, of course, leaves unanswered a more fundamental question; why have a category of restitution for wrongs at all? The answer is not immediately obvious. Certainly, the fact that you are richer as a result of having wronged me will not do on its own. Grant that you do not deserve to keep profit made as a result of wronging me: this does not show that I should have any right to claim it from you, particularly if I cannot show any other specific ground of liability (e.g. duress or mistake) to justify recovery. Indeed, there is a good case for arguing that once a man has paid for any losses his activities cause, *prima facie* he ought in a free society to be able to go about his business without further hindrance; the law ought not, without strong justification, to go further and insist that he justify his retention of the other assets he happens to have.

11-04   In fact there would seem to be three broad cases where restitution for wrongs is justified. One (reflecting what can be called the 'property benefit principle') comes from our general understanding of ownership, and arises where the essence of the plaintiff's claim is profit made by the defendant from some asset of his. If I own a mare I ought to own any foals it produces. By parity of reasoning, is it not clear that if you take my mare and wrongfully hire it out, thus causing it to produce financial rather than biological progeny, or if you take the opportunity of your position as a trustee looking after it to make a profit out of it, I should have a claim to that gain as well? And if so with a horse, why not with any other kind of property?

The second case where restitution is called for - representing what will be called the 'anti-enrichment wrong' principle - is where the duty broken by the defendant is one that is imposed on him specifically to prevent him making a profit, rather than (as is normally the case) simply to protect the other party from loss.

The third - and perhaps the most doubtful - is the 'prophylactic' case: people should not be encouraged to infringe others' rights, and to that end, even if the plaintiff does not deserve the defendant's profit, he should have the right to claim it to discourage the defendant from making it in the first place.

We now deal with the various heads of restitution for wrongs.

1 TORTS

There is no general cause of action for the profit gained by **11-05**
committing a tort; a tort action *prima facie* lies for loss alone. Nevertheless,
there are exceptions.

The availability of exemplary damages

In libel, slander, trespass, assault, false imprisonment and malicious **11-06**
prosecution, exemplary damages may be given over and above any
pecuniary or other losses suffered. This is possible where the defendant is
proved to have been a knowing wrongdoer, and to have acted with the
aim of making a profit even after taking into account any damages
payable[3]. This principle, which will not be extended[4], approximates to a
rough and ready form of restitution: tort, at least to this extent, should
not pay[5]. The similarities, however, should not be exaggerated;
particularly since, although this liability is dependent on the making of a
profit, the amount payable by the defendant is not limited to the amount
of profit made. No nice arithmetical calculation need be made; provided
any award amounts to condign punishment for the defendant, it will not
be interfered with on appeal[6]. Furthermore, the specific limitation to
knowing wrongdoing, and to acts done with the intent of making a
profit[7], suggest a penal rather than a restitutionary background; indeed, it
is arguable that this whole facet of exemplary damages is really just an
anomalous extension of the criminal law into the law of tort.

Damages: gain masquerading as loss

Suppose I borrow your car and return it a week late; suppose further **11-07**
that during that time you would not in fact have used it. Damages in
conversion are at large, and may in suitable cases be measured not by
your loss, which is nil, but at the reasonable hire value of the car for the

---

[3] *Rookes v. Barnard* [1964] A.C. 1129, 1226 (Lord Devlin); *Broome v. Cassell* [1972] A.C. 1027, 1073 (Lord Hailsham).

[4] *Rookes v. Barnard* [1964] A.C. 1129, 1221 (Lord Devlin); *A.B. v. South West Water* [1993] 1 All E.R. 609.

[5] E.g. *Drane v. Evangelou* [1978] 2 All E.R. 437.

[6] E.g. *Broome v. Cassell* [1972] A.C. 1027; *Drane v. Evangelou* [1978] 2 All E.R. 437.

[7] The mere fact that in the nature of things a newspaper printing a libellous story of considerable public interest may expect some increase in circulation will not do: *Broadway Approvals v. Odham's Press* [1965] 2 All E.R. 523.

extra period[8]. Similar principles apply to trespass to land: if I repeatedly drive my vehicles over your land in the course of my business, or use it as a dumping ground for my waste, I may be liable to you not simply for any damage I do but for a reasonable sum by way of wayleave or dumping charge[9]. Yet again, damages for infringement of patent or copyright, or for misuse of confidential commercial information, are not infrequently assessed at the sum the infringer might reasonably have expected to have to pay by way of royalty[10].

This particular way of measuring damages is, however, in its nature limited to torts involving infringement of property rights and the like (including intellectual property); the idea of a reasonable charge for permission to commit other torts, such as libel or assault, is hardly attractive. Furthermore, it is of course only partly restitutionary, since it lies for a reasonable fee and not for the actual profit made. If, in the course of the extra week when I had kept your car, I had hired it out for double the hire charge I could have expected to pay, I should still only have had to pay the latter by way of damages (but see waiver of tort, below).

Waiver of tort

11-08   In contrast to the previous two causes of action, where restitution comes in (as it were) interstitially, in certain cases a tort victim can, by a process known as 'waiver of tort'[11], elect to claim not his loss but the cash proceeds gained by the defendant. (The cause of action is, technically, money had and received, and is a distinct cause of action from that for the tort itself[12]).

The commonest use of waiver of tort is in connection with the wrongful sale or use of goods: the plaintiff can waive the tort of conversion and elect to claim the actual amount paid to the defendant rather than the value of what was converted[13]. But it is not limited to

---

[8]   *Strand Electric Co. v. Brisford Entertainments* [1952] 2 Q.B. 246; *Hillesden Securities v. Ryjack* [1983] 2 All E.R. 184. But see *Saleh Farid v. Theodorou* (unreported, C.A., 30 January 1992).

[9]   *Jegon v. Vivian* (1871) L.R. 6 Ch. App. 742; *Whitwham v. Westminster Brymbo Coal Co.* [1892] 2 Ch. 538; *cf Swordheath Properties v. Tabet* [1979] 1 All E.R. 240, 242.

[10]   E.g. *General Tire v. Firestone* [1975] 2 All E.R. 173 (patent); *Stovin-Bradford v. Volpoint* [1971] 3 All E.R. 571 (copyright).

[11]   'Waiver' not in the sense that the plaintiff condones or forgives the wrong, but because he must elect between this cause of action and one for damages *tout court*. See *United Australia v. Barclays Bank* [1941] A.C. 1.

[12]   See e.g. *Morris v. Tarrant* [1971] 2 Q.B. 143 (action for proceeds of goods converted not subject to same limitation period as action in conversion proper).

[13]   E.g. *Hambly v. Trott* (1776) 1 Cowp. 371.

conversion; it can apply equally – though perhaps with less justification – to the seduction of a menial servant[14], and to deceit[15]. The right is not dependent on knowledge by the defendant of the wrongfulness of his act.

Most cases of waiver of tort have hitherto been for straightforward money profit. There is no reason on principle, however, why it should not extend to other sorts of gains, such as items of property[16], or saving of inevitable expenditure. On the other hand, it is unlikely whether on present authority it would. In *Phillips v. Homfray*[17] the defendant unlawfully led coal over the plaintiff's property. An attempt was made to waive the tort of trespass[18] and recover from the defendant's estate the expense thus saved; but this failed, partly on the ground that such negative savings could not form the subject of an action for money had and received.

Can the principle be extended to further torts not hitherto covered? On present English authority this must be doubtful. There is clear authority against extending it to trespass to land. Here damages can, in certain instances, reflect profits anyway; and according to the decision in *Phillips v. Homfray*[19], the victim must claim the trespasser's profit under this head or not at all. In view of the strict limitations on exemplary damages in, say, libel, it is most unlikely that the courts will countenance any general right to waive that tort. Indeed, since the refusal by the Court of Appeal in *A.B. v. South West Water Services*[20] to extend exemplary damages beyond the torts for which they had traditionally been awarded (the tort in issue there being nuisance), it is likely that the courts will not allow this principle to be outflanked by similar attempts to extend the range of torts that can be waived. It is also worth remembering that in the case of intellectual property rights the remedy of account of profits has long been available[21]: if so, it is even more likely that the courts will think there is no general need for a cause of action for actual profits made from wrongdoing.

11-09

Moreover, it is respectfully suggested that this reluctance is right. Exemplary damages apart (and accepted as anomalous), the torts where some remedy is available to the plaintiff against the profits made by the

---

[14] E.g. *Lightly v. Clouston* (1808) 1 Taunt 112.

[15] *Madden v. Kempster* (1807) 1 Camp 12; *Hill v. Perrott* (1810) 3 Taunt 274. But in any case is not the money recoverable as money paid by mistake?

[16] See *Hill v. Perrott* (1810) 3 Taunt 274 (goods delivered as a result of fraud).

[17] (1883) 24 Ch. D. 439.

[18] As the law then stood, the plaintiff could not take the understandable course and sue for a reasonable wayleave by way of damages, since the defendant was dead. Today he could (see Law Reform (Miscellaneous Provisions) Act 1934, s. 1(1)); and so the point of waiver of tort would not arise.

[19] (1883) 24 Ch. D. 439.

[20] [1993] 1 All E.R. 609.

[21] See generally A. Burrows, *Remedies for Torts and Breach of Contract*, p.263 ff.

defendant are broadly those connected with the protection of property[22], i.e. aimed at preventing the defendant from enriching himself by using that which is not his. Elsewhere, at least in the absence of knowing wrongdoing, there is less call for stripping the defendant of his gains.

11-10   What if there is knowing wrongdoing? It is sometimes suggested that, quite apart from the above liabilities, there ought to be a right to recover profits deliberately made from intentional wrongdoing, whatever the cause of action involved. Furthermore, it is true that the presence or absence of deliberate wrongdoing may affect the grant of an account of profits[23]. But, with respect, this is by no means obvious. True, if you are paid £1,000 to beat me up you do not deserve to keep the £1,000; but then, why should I have it? Despite one's intuitive feeling, it is very difficult to say that the £1,000 is genuinely gained at my expense so as to justify giving me a cause of action to sue you for it. If it is to be taken away from you it should be done by the criminal law and not at all.

Conversion and tracing

11-11   To the coverage above must be added one feature of so-called 'common-law tracing' (above, Chapter 10). Where a thief or mala fide receiver of my property exchanges it for something else, it is (apparently) open to me adopt the exchange, if I so wish, and claim ownership of the product. So if you steal my sheep and exchange it for a goat I can claim to be the owner of the goat while it is in your hands. This, at least, seems to be the result of *Taylor v. Plumer*[24]. A broker stole his principal's money and changed it into bearer bonds: the principal traced him, caught him and forcibly repossessed the bonds. He was held justified in doing so, on the basis that he could choose to adopt the exchange and hence regard the bonds as his own. But note that this principle only applies while the product is in the deliberate wrongdoer's hands. Once it has reached the hands of a bona fide recipient X, whether for value or not, the owner cannot exercise his rights so as to make X a wrongdoer[25].

---

[22] Though admittedly not exclusively; waiver of deceit is difficult to fit into this scheme. On the other hand, it has been suggested above that the need for this is problematical anyway, given the right to sue for money paid by mistake.

[23] As in *Seager v. Copydex* [1967] 2 All E.R. 415, 419 (breach of confidence), cited by P. Birks, *Introduction to the Law of Restitution*, 345; see too *Young v. Holt* (1947) 65 R.P.C. 25 (passing-off). But this is hardly a strong foundation for a general principle: compare Copyright, Designs and Patents Act 1988, s. 97(1), in which certain innocent infringers of copyright are not liable in damages but are liable to an account of profits!

[24] (1815) 3 M & S 562.

[25] See e.g. *Commercial Banking Co. of Sydney v. Mann* [1961] A.C. 1.

2 BREACH OF CONTRACT

As with tort, so with contract; if I can break my contract with you, **11-12**
pay you damages and still come out with a profit, that is my good luck.
Prima facie[26], there is nothing you can do to extract that profit from me[27].
Indeed I do rather better, since unlike tort, breach of contract cannot give
rise to exemplary damages.

Again, however, as with tort, there are exceptions to this principle.

Contracts providing for payment over of profits

It seems there is no objection to a contract providing expressly or **11-13**
impliedly that certain acts are not to be done without the consent of one
or other party, and that if there are any profits they must be paid over to
that party[28]. A neat example is a contract of agency: an agent who takes a
bribe is guilty of a breach of contract, and has simply on this account to
pay it over to his principal, quite apart from any liability for breach of
fiduciary duty[29].

Breach of contract amounting to misuse of property

Suppose you agree to let me leave my car in your garage for a week **11-14**
for £10; in breach of contract I leave it there for a fortnight. According
to the decision in *Penarth Dock v. Pounds*[30], your measure of damages is
analogous to that in tort for trespass or conversion, i.e. the reasonable hire
value of the garage for the extra week, independently of what in fact you
would have done with it.

Breach of contract not to do something without consent

Assume a restrictive covenant prevents you building in your garden **11-15**
without my consent; you nevertheless do so. It seems I can get damages
based on the profit you made from your breach of covenant (normally

---

[26] Unless, of course, you have some other independent ground of restitution. A vendor of real
property who wrongfully sells it to a third party at a profit has to account for that profit to the
purchaser; but this results not from his breach of contract but from the fact that he held the
subject-matter on constructive trust for the purchaser.

[27] E.g. *Tito v. Waddell (No. 2)* [1977] Ch. 106, 332 (Megarry V-C); *Surrey CC v. Bredero Homes*
[1993] 3 All ER 705.

[28] *Quaere*, though, what the effect of the law on penalty clauses would be on this.

[29] E.g. *Industries & General Mortgage Co. v. Lewis* [1949] 2 All E.R. 573.

[30] [1963] 1 Lloyds Rep. 359.

reckoned as the sum I could reasonably have asked from you as the price of release[31]), provided two conditions are met. These are that (1) an injunction was on principle available at the time I brought my action; and (2) I actually sought that remedy, even though I may not have got it[32]. Although this can be explained as involving a kind of loss suffered by me (i.e. the loss of my ability to demand a sum not to stop you building) this is not very convincing: if my right is one in respect of which an injunction would not in fact have been granted, it is a little difficult to see that I could have charged anything substantial for releasing it.

As with the profiteering deliberate tortfeasor, it has often been suggested that the present treatment of the 'cynical' contract-breaker is wrong, and that he ought to come under an independent liability to account for his profits[33]. But this is subject to the same objection as before: however little the contract-breaker may deserve those profits, it is not clear that the victim has a better claim to them. Indeed, this can be argued *a fortiori* in the case of contract-breakers; whereas tortfeasors encounter each other willy-nilly, contractors can always stipulate beforehand what is to happen to any incidental profits. If they do not, gains, like losses, should lie where they fall.

3 BREACH OF TRUST OR FIDUCIARY DUTY

11-16   Turning from breach of contract and tort to breach of trustees' and other fiduciary duties, the contrast is striking: the duty to account for profits wrongly made suddenly stops being an anomaly and becomes the norm. This disparate treatment of what are, at bottom, simply different species of wrong is at first sight odd: but on closer inspection it becomes a good deal more understandable. The specific cases of tort and breach of contract that give rise to duties of restitution are largely (though admittedly not exclusively) concerned with unlawful interference with property rights, or with express or implied duties specifically aimed at prevention of unwarranted profits. Now, in tort and contract such things are the exception; in fiduciary relations, by contrast, they are much more the norm. Trusts are about the duty to look after, and hence not profit from, misusing others' assets. The duties of agents, company directors, partners, and others normally reckoned to be in a fiduciary position are duties not only to serve those others' interests but to provide unbiased judgment in doing so. If so, it is hardly surprising that the law should be

---

31 See *Wrotham Park Estates v. Parkside Homes* [1974] 2 All E.R. 321.

32 Conditions imposed by Ferris J in *Surrey County Council v. Bredero Homes* [1992] 3 All E.R. 302, affirmed [1993] 3 All E.R. 705.

33 Birks, *Introduction to the Law of Restitution*, 334 ff; Jones (1983) 99 L.Q.R. 443.

so willing to impose on such people a *prima facie* duty not to profit from their position, and to pay over any gains when they do, and that further it should give their beneficiaries title to sue for restitution of it.

Trustees

Prima facie a trustee who makes any profit out of the trust property   **11-17**
itself, or from his position in relation to it[34], commits a wrong, and must pay this over to his beneficiary. In this connection it does not matter whether the trustee acted honestly or otherwise[35]; nor, since we are talking here about restitution for wrongs, is it relevant that the profit could not have gone to the beneficiaries at all[36]. A similar principle attaches to an adviser to a trustee or other third party who makes use of such an opportunity, presumably on the basis that he is a joint wrongdoer and can be in no better position than the trustee himself. The notorious decision in *Phipps v. Boardman*[37] illustrates neatly both the principle and its extent. An adviser to a trust discovered that a company in which the trust held shares was badly managed; there was little doubt that large profits could be made by taking it over and reconstructing it. The trust being unable to provide all the necessary capital, the adviser put up part of it himself. He was held liable to repay to the beneficiaries[38] the profit made on his own money: though he was, to be fair, allowed to set off a sum reflecting his own expenditure of time and skill[39].

It is not difficult to justify the trustee's liability as regards profit made   **11-18**
from use of actual trust property (e.g. my trustee depositing trust shares as security in order to make a spectacularly successful investment); this clearly comes under the property principle. But what about other cases involving mere opportunity – for instance, where the trustee's successful investment came merely from information received as such? Unless one squares the circle by saying all opportunities of this sort count as property anyway[40], this is much trickier. Prophylaxis and anti-enrichment

---

[34] E.g. the trustee being paid as a director of a company in which the trust holds shares: *Re Macadam* [1946] Ch. 73.

[35] See *Phipps v. Boardman* [1967] 2 A.C. 46, a classic case of an honest and well-meaning defendant being held liable.

[36] *Keech v. Sandford* (1726) 1 Eq. Cas. Abr. 741; *Phipps v. Boardman*, above; *cf IDC v. Cooley* (1972) 2 All E.R. 162. See too the Australian decision in *Chan v. Zacharia* (1984) 154 C.L.R. 178, where Deane J said a fiduciary had to account for benefits received if either they arose from the fiduciary's position, or they arose from a possible conflict of interest and duty.

[37] [1967] 2 A.C. 46.

[38] Except, of course, those who had consented.

[39] Which, for obvious reasons, he would not have been allowed to do had he been guilty of knowing wrongdoing: *cf Guinness plc. v. Saunders* [1990] 1 All E.R. 652.

[40] As was apparently done by two members of the House of Lords in *Phipps v. Boardman* [1967] 2 A.C. 46; see pp.107 (Lord Hodson) and 115 (Lord Guest). The other members of the house were not prepared to do this; see pp.89–90 (Lord Dilhorne), 102 (Lord Cohen), 127–128 (Lord Upjohn).

obviously have something to do with it; a trustee's duty to give unbiased attention to trust matters may entail a duty to avoid making incidental profits and to hand them over if they are made, and could perhaps justify rules to encourage him never to put himself in a position where his impartiality might be compromised. Nevertheless, they cannot explain or justify the whole rule. To regard making a profit out of trust information as an anti-enrichment wrong even where there was no element of bad faith and the profit could not have gone to the trust anyway, is (it is suggested) going too far; and the prophylaxis argument is not very convincing when extended to conduct that shows no impropriety and that is incapable of harming the interests of the beneficiary.

Other fiduciaries

11-19   The category of fiduciaries is a notoriously wide and varied one. It runs from those, like personal representatives and – to a lesser extent – company directors, who are treated very like trustees, to others, such as agents, mortgagees, joint tenants and partners, whose duties are far more limited. Fiduciaries, in other words, vary greatly in their legal treatment[41]. All on principle, however, owe a duty not to make a profit out of their position. In the case of personal representatives, directors and agents, this is presumably on the same basis as trustees, i.e. their beneficiaries' need for dispassionate advice or dealing. Hence cases such as *Regal (Hastings) Ltd. v. Gulliver*[42], holding company directors liable to pay over profits in a situation highly analogous to that in *Phipps v. Boardman*[43]. Again, if I employ you as my agent I have a right to expect that you will exercise judgment unclouded by possibilities of personal advantage from bribes and the like; hence my right to claim from you, without question, any bribe or other secret profit you receive in the course of so acting[44]. On the other hand, the relation of principal and agent has been held to permit the retention of certain benefits by the agent that, while coming to him by virtue of his position, have nothing to do with the relations between him and his principal[45].

11-20   It is suggested, moreover, that breach of fiduciary duty, like breach of a trustee's duty, is an 'anti-enrichment' wrong giving rise to restitution not only as against the fiduciary himself but also as against anyone else knowingly participating in it. *Arab Monetary Fund v. Hashim*[46] makes this

---

[41] *Cf* in another context, *Re Coomber* [1911] 1 Ch. 723.

[42] [1942] 1 All E.R. 378.

[43] [1967] 2 A.C. 46.

[44] As in *Boston Deep Sea Fishing v. Ansell* (1888) 39 Ch. D. 339.

[45] E.g. *Aas v. Benham* [1891] 2 Ch. 244; *NZ Netherlands Society v. Kuys* [1973] 1 W.L.R. 1126.

[46] [1993] 1 Lloyds Rep. 543, esp. at 565.

reasoning clear. Builders obtained a valuable contract by bribing the building owners' agent; having performed it and been paid, they were held liable to pay over the amount of the bribe to the owners on the basis that they had participated in a breach of fiduciary duty and that the amount of the bribe must be regarded as representing extra profits made as a result of so doing.

This leaves one slightly problematical category of fiduciaries: partners **11-21** and mortgagees. It is clear that they too come under fiduciary duties[47]: but why? Arguably the reason is the same as with other fiduciaries, i.e. that all breaches of fiduciary duty, including those attaching to partners and the like, are fundamentally anti-enrichment wrongs. On this reasoning, by becoming a partner or mortgagee, one undertakes to conduct the business or utilise the asset concerned for the collective profit rather than individual advantage. On the other hand, this may be regarded as unreal; on balance it might well be better to base the duties placed on partners and mortgagees squarely on the 'property principle'. Mortgaged property and partnership business should arguably be regarded as belonging to a sort of collectivity rather than simply to the individual owners; it is therefore the former, rather than the latter, that should have the advantage of any profit from it.

4 INTELLECTUAL PROPERTY

By long tradition, infringements of intellectual property rights are **11-22** always regarded as anti-enrichment wrongs. This is given effect to by the peculiar remedy of account of profits. Originally a purely equitable creation, this is now available by statute for breach of copyright[48] and patent[49]; in cases of breach of confidence[50], passing-off[51] and trade mark infringement[52] the original judge-made right still has to be invoked. It is a discretionary remedy, alternative to damages[53], and may be refused on any of the usual equitable grounds[54].

A troublesome point here is how far a defendant should escape liability to account for profits if he did not know, and had no reason to know, he

---

[47] E.g. *Thompson's Trustee v. Heaton* [1974] 1 All E.R. 1239 (partners); *Nelson v. Hannam* [1943] Ch. 59 (mortgagees).

[48] Copyright, Designs and Patents Act 1988, s. 96(2).

[49] Patents Act 1977, s. 61(1)(d).

[50] E.g. *Peter Pan Mfg. Co. v. Corsets Silhouette* [1963] 3 All E.R. 402.

[51] E.g. *Weingarten v. Bayer* (1903) 22 R.P.C. 341.

[52] *Kerly's Law of Trade Marks and Trade Names*, 12th ed., §15-80.

[53] *Sutherland v. Caxton* [1936] Ch. 323, 336.

[54] *Van Zeller v. Mason Catley* (1907) 25 R.P.C. 37; *Young v. Holt* (1947) 65 R.P.C. 25.

was infringing the plaintiff's rights (except, that is, with patents, where by statute a person who escapes liability to damages on account of innocence also avoids liability to an account of profits[55]). Logically, it is suggested that liability to account for profits should be strict, as *prima facie* is liability to pay damages. If a wrong is indeed categorised an 'anti-enrichment' wrong, the defendant's enrichment from committing it remains unjustified, however innocent he was; indeed, it may be easier to justify making the innocent defendant account for profits than pay damages since the former remedy, at least in theory, cannot leave him out of pocket. This principle is indeed observed in copyright and design right, so much so that in at least one case liability to account for profits is actually wider than that for damages[56]. On the other hand, in trade mark infringement, passing off and breach of confidence, the innocence of the defendant seems, for no convincing justification, to be regarded as a reason for the court to exercise its discretion against granting an account[57].

5 RESTITUTIONARY REMEDIES AVAILABLE FOR WRONGS

Form

11-23   Subject to a few exceptions, there is no doubt that restitution for wrongs takes the form of a simple money liability, whether it takes the form of damages, account of profits or money had and received; there is no question of the claimant being able to claim equitable ownership of the unwarranted profit or priority in insolvency.

The exceptions

Taylor v. Plumer

11-24   We mentioned above that if you steal my horse and exchange it for a cow I have the right under the rule in *Taylor v. Plumer*[58] to claim ownership of the cow while it is in your hands. Since this liability of yours depends on your being a wrongdoer, this provides a *de facto* exception to the above principle.

---

[55] Patents Act 1977, s. 62(1).

[56] See Copyright, Designs and Patents Act 1988, ss. 97(1).

[57] See *Seager v. Copydex* [1967] 2 All E.R. 415, 419 (breach of confidence), *Young v. Holt* [1947] 65 R.P.C. 25 (passing-off).

[58] (1815) 3 M & S 562.

'Property benefits'

The fact that your gain arose from the disposal, use or exploitation of **11-25** something belonging to me not only provides a reason to make you accountable for that gain; it also often justifies giving me the remedies of an owner against it while it remains in your hands. If I lend you my car and you sell it, not only are you liable to me for the price you got for it: while you still have the money in your hands, you will hold it on constructive trust for me[59]. Similarly (it is submitted) where you borrow my car and without my consent hire it out to a stranger: the hire fees, while you still have them, ought to be held on trust for me.

Similarly, too, with equitable interests: there has been no doubt since *Keech v. Sandford*[60] that where a trustee or other fiduciary makes a profit either from using trust property, or by virtue of his legal ownership of it, he will hold that profit on constructive trust for the beneficiary, and will not simply come under a duty to account. Although most of the cases have concerned peripheral matters such as the renewal of trust leases or the purchase of reversions thereto, there is no doubt that similar reasoning would apply to, e.g. a trustee who hired out trust property.

Other fiduciary profits

Suppose you, a trustee, make a profit not by using actual trust property **11-26** but merely by virtue of your position as trustee; for instance (as in *Phipps v. Boardman*[61]) by using information that has come to you as such. Or suppose that, in the course of acting as my agent, you receive a large bribe from a third party. Should the 'property benefit' reasoning be extended to situations of this sort, so as to make you not only accountable – which you clearly ought to be – but a constructive trustee of any gains made?

In *Phipps's* case itself the original order made, declaring a trust, suggested the answer yes[62]. And in the very important case of *Att-Gen* for *Hong Kong v. Reid*[63] the Privy Council decided that this indeed was so. Hence, where a public prosecutor in Hong Kong received massive bribes and invested the proceeds in freehold properties in New Zealand, it was

---

[59]   *Cf Clough Mill v. Martin* [1984] 3 All E.R. 982 and the other 'retention of title' cases.

[60]   (1726) 1 Eq. Cas. Abr. 741; more recently, *Protheroe v. Protheroe* [1968] 1 All E.R. 1111 and *Thompson's Trustee v. Heaton* [1974] 1 All E.R. 1239.

[61]   [1967] 2 A.C. 46.

[62]   But no argument was presented on this aspect either in the Court of Appeal or the House of Lords. Nor did it matter in that case, since the defendant was perfectly solvent and the measure of recovery was the same in either case.

[63]   (1993) 143 New L.J. 1569. This case overruled the long-standing earlier decision in *Lister v. Stubbs* (1890) 45 Ch. D. 1, where it had been held that an agent receiving a bribe was merely under a personal duty to account.

held that those properties were held in their entirety on trust for the Hong Kong Government.

The reasoning underlying this conclusion is not hard to see. After all, why distinguish between profiteers according to whether they misused others' property or merely abused their own position? Again, the distinction between a trust and a duty to account principally matters where the profiteer is insolvent and the argument is between beneficiary and creditors: if so, why should creditors be allowed to benefit from money their debtor should never have had in the first place? And yet again, suppose the fiduciary, having made his profit, invests cannily and increases it: should the beneficiary not have a claim against this futher gain?

11-27 On the other hand, it must be said that there are also strong arguments against the conclusion reached in *Reid's* case. In order to allow a proprietary claim, whether by way of constructive trust or otherwise, against property in a defendant's hands, one has normally to start with some proprietary base. To make sense of such a claim, should I not have to be able to show that the assets in your possession derive from something I do, or did, own?

Nor are the policy arguments entirely one-sided. Distinctions between property and other claimants are as old as the law itself, and can hardly be objectionable as such; to take one example from the law of restitution itself, if you make a profit from selling my goods I can claim it in specie, whereas if you profit from libelling me I have to be satisfied with a personal claim in respect of your gain. So too with the argument that creditors should not gain from what their bankrupt debtor should not have had: no-one has ever suggested that this reasoning should be applied, e.g. to the seller who is paid for goods but then goes bankrupt before supplying them[64]. As for the argument that the fiduciary should have to pay over not only profit but profit on profit, this may well be true; but there are other ways of reaching that result than by inventing a bogus proprietary claim. Arguably a better solution would have been to say that the fiduciary is only under a personal liability, but that that liability extends not only to immediate profits, but also to all subsequent gains resulting from it, provided they are not too remote[65].

Profits and losses

11-28 Where benefits can be recovered on the ground that they were gained as a result of a wrongful act, a further question arises: is this right cumulative with, or alternative to, the victim's right to claim his loss? As a

---

64 Cf *Eldan Services v. Chandag Motors* (1990) 3 All E.R. 459.

65 As suggested by Professor Birks before *Reid* was decided: see his *Introduction to the Law of Restitution*, 387 ff.

matter of policy, something can be said on both sides. To allow cumulation over-compensates plaintiffs: on the other hand, it is a little odd to treat in the same way a defendant who gains while causing the plaintiff no loss, and one who in addition causes some loss, but still less than the amount of his gain. Nevertheless, the general rule seems to be against cumulation. This is clear in the case of the equitable remedy of account of profits[66]; and elsewhere the Privy Council has made it clear that a defaulting fiduciary can be sued for his profits or for the beneficiary's loss, but not both[67]. Presumably a trustee is in the same position. As for waiver of tort, it is well-established that where it is available, is an alternative to an action for damages; the plaintiff has to elect which he wants[68]. On the other hand, this is not an absolute rule: where exemplary damages in tort are allowed, these are traditionally awarded over and above any sum for loss suffered[69].

---

[66] *Sutherland v. Caxton* [1936] Ch. 323, 336.

[67] *Mahesan v. Malaysia Government Housing Society* [1979] A.C. 374.

[68] *United Australia v. Barclays Bank* [1941] A.C. 1, 18.

[69] Thus in *Broome v. Cassell* [1972] A.C. 1027 £15,000 was awarded for compensation and £25,000 in addition by way of exemplary damages.

CHAPTER 12

SUBROGATION

Subrogation involves the transfer of the beneficial title to an asset by operation of law. The asset transferred is normally either the benefit of a claim, such as a debt or right of action in tort, or alternatively some charge or other interest – such as a mortgage or an unpaid vendor's lien – over another's property. When subrogation takes place, the right can be enforced by the transferee[1]; furthermore, any product of it – such as monies recovered in respect of a right of action in tort – equally belongs to him in equity[2]. The purpose of the transfer is very often to reverse unjust enrichment: in some cases that of the person from whom the benefit of the asset is transferred[3], in others (more commonly if less obviously), that of the debtor or chargor, who would otherwise get an unjustified windfall[4].

12-01

There is room for argument over whether subrogation is best regarded as a remedy or an independent head of restitutionary recovery. The view taken here is that the latter is the better view: although in one case (that of sureties and those regarded as analogous to sureties), subrogation parallels other restitutionary rights, elsewhere it very definitely extends them by providing restitution where none would otherwise exist.

12-02

The right to subrogation may, of course, be abandoned or excluded by contract[5]: it has been suggested that the court has a more general discretion to disallow it where it is not just and equitable[6], but with respect this seems unlikely.

Subrogation arises in a number of fairly disparate situations, but four call for particular comment. These are: (1) its use as an extension to equitable tracing; (2) where money lent and otherwise irrecoverable is used to pay off valid obligations of the borrower; (3) in principal and surety and similar situations; and (4) in insurance. There is little in common between them, and each is worth briefly dealing with separately.

---

[1] Subject, normally, to the necessity to join the transferor as a party to the action: *Mason v. Sainsbury* (1782) 3 Doug K.B. 61.

[2] *Lord Napier & Ettrick v. Hunter* [1993] 1 All E.R. 385.

[3] As with the insurer's right to be subrogated to the assured's rights against third parties.

[4] As in the case of the plaintiff whose money goes to pay off some obligation affecting the defendant's property.

[5] As was held to be the case in *Morris v. Ford Motor Co.* (1973) 2 All E.R. 1084.

[6] *Morris v. Ford Motor Co.* [1973] 2 All E.R. 1084, 1090, *per* Lord Denning MR.

1 EXTENDING EQUITABLE TRACING

12-03   We saw in Chapter 10 above that, in so far as property in which I
have an equitable interest is transformed into an asset in your hands, so
that you end up positively enriched, I have a claim by substitution to that
asset. Subrogation mirrors this process where my property enriches you,
but only negatively, by going to discharge some obligation of yours (e.g.
where you use it to pay off a mortgage on your house)[7].

The rules relating to identification - i.e. what property in your hands
represents that which was mine - are the same as for equitable tracing.
The right to subrogate, however, is subject to one vital qualification, even
assuming that those rules are satisfied: for whereas equitable tracing is
always available against the volunteer recipient, however unknowing, the
innocent volunteer who negatively enriches himself by using another's
property to discharge an obligation or charge on his own property is
immune to any remedy. The reason is the rather unconvincing one that
the volunteer's use of the money or other property amounts to a change
of position justifying refusal of restitutionary relief[8]. In practice, therefore,
this is a rather limited type of relief.

2 MONEY LENT AND OTHERWISE IRRECOVERABLE AND/OR LENT ON UNENFORCEABLE SECURITY

12-04   Loans made to borrowers, or security taken for them, may often turn
out to be ineffective or unenforceable, whether by statute or otherwise[9].
While no doubt there are good social reasons for this, it obviously leads
to possibilities of serious unjustified enrichment, whether of the recipient
of the loan (where he gets the benefit without having to pay it back), or
his general creditors (where they, rather than the would-be secured
creditor, get the benefit of the property that should have gone to secure
the obligation). Not surprisingly, in a number of situations the law takes
the view that something must be done about this.

The difficulty is, of course, that one cannot simply allow a
restitutionary claim here without running the risk of subverting the very

---

[7]   *Cf Re Diplock* [1948] Ch. 465 at p.530. The reason subrogation was not allowed against the
charities who had used funds to pay off secured obligations was that they had done so in all
innocence. Had the circumstances been otherwise there can be little doubt the remedy would
have been available.

[8]   *Re Diplock* [1948] Ch. 465, 521, 549.

[9]   Agents' unauthorised borrowings and *ultra vires* loans to corporations are the chief non-
statutory categories.

rules of law that made the original loan or security ineffective in the first place. A narrower remedy is therefore needed, and this can be provided by subrogation. Where the loan concerned is used to pay off other enforceable obligations binding on the borrower, or to discharge securities binding on his property, the lender is in certain cases entitled to take over the rights of the previous creditor or security holder.

But why go even this far, since the effect is to allow enforcement of an otherwise ineffective transaction? The explanation that the plaintiff is founding, not on his own right, but on another's claim which he has taken over, is true but unhelpful; we still have to explain why he has been allowed to take the benefit of that other claim. More convincing, it is suggested, is the argument that if the law merely substitutes one creditor for another the defendant does not, in the event, lose out[10]. (On the other hand, it is difficult to see the logic of acceding to this argument in the subrogation cases and not extending it to all cases where the defendant has benefited from the loan and cannot claim change of position in good faith).

Unenforceable loans

Where a loan is irrecoverable from the borrower by reason of minority, **12-05**
or the doctrine of *ultra vires*, or lack of authority, it is clear that, in so far as the money advanced is actually used to pay off valid and enforceable debts, the lender is entitled to stand in the shoes of those paid off. So a 16-year-old who borrows money cannot be made to pay it back: but if he uses it to pay for necessaries he can be made liable to the lender to that extent through subrogation[11]. A corporation borrowing *ultra vires* can be sued to the extent that the monies so borrowed were expended on valid debts owed by it[12]. Again, in *Bannatyne v. MacIver*[13] an agent without authority borrowed funds, and with authority used them to pay his principal's debts; the principal was held liable to repay. Similarly, a bank paying a customer's cheque without a mandate to do so can defend any action by the customer in so far as such payments went to pay off enforceable obligations owed by the customer to third parties[14]. It does not seem to matter whether the borrower was bound by contract to use the sum advanced to pay off the

---

[10] 'The test is, Has the transaction really added to the liabilities of the campany [borrowing *ultra vires*]?' - *Blackburn Benefit B.S. v. Cunliffe Brooks & Co.* (1882) 22 Ch. D. 61, 71 (Lord Selborne).

[11] E.g. *Marlow v. Pitfeild* (1719) 1 P. Wms. 558. See too *Re National Permanent B.S.* (1869) L.R. 5 Ch. App. 309, 313.

[12] E.g. *Wenlock v. River Dee Co.* (1887) 19 Q.B.D. 155; *cf Re Wrexham, Mold & Connah's Quay Ry* [1899] 1 Ch. 440.

[13] [1906] 1 K.B. 103.

[14] *Liggett v. Barclays Bank* [1928] 1 K.B. 48.

other obligation concerned[15], or even whether the creditor knew of the irrecoverability of the loan. What matters is simply the actual use to which the money was put[16]: to that extent, the law seems happy to give a windfall to the lucky would-be creditor.

12–06   On the other hand, the lender can never normally use the doctrine of subrogation to put himself into a better situation than he would have been in had his loan been enforceable in the ordinary way. Hence if he intended to make an unsecured loan, but the monies were used to discharge a secured obligation, the lender cannot take over the security[17]: he merely takes over a personal claim[18] against the borrower. But even this principle is subject to exceptions. One advancing money to pay the crew of a ship is apparently entitled to be subrogated to the latter's maritime lien without regard to whether he intended to lend secured[19]; and by statute a person advancing money, even unsecured, to a company to pay wages is subrogated to the rights of the workers so paid ahead of other creditors in the event of the company going into liquidation[20].

Unenforceable security

12–07   Where the lender intended a secured loan, but for some reason the security was ineffective, he may be subrogated to any securities discharged with the proceeds. A neat example is *Thurstan v. Nottingham Permanent Building Society*[21]. Lenders lent a minor money to buy land from X (whom they paid directly), at the same time taking a mortgage from the minor. Although the mortgage was ineffective, the lenders successfully claimed subrogation to X's unpaid vendor's lien. Similar principles have been applied where secured loans entered into without authority were used to pay off other charges that were binding on the purported borrower[22].

Note, however, that this is subject to two important qualifications. First, it seems that (unlike the case of unenforceable loans) it is not enough that the borrower actually used the monies to pay off the other

---

[15] *Cf Wenlock v. River Dee Co.* (1887) 19 QBD 155, where the money advanced went to pay debts contracted after the loan concerned. But *cf* the case where the claimant seeks to be subrogated to a security rather than to a mere personal claim: *Wylie v. Carlyon* [1922] 1 Ch. 51, below.

[16] *Blackburn Benefit B.S. v. Cunliffe Brooks & Co.* (1882) 22 Ch. D. 61.

[17] *Re Wrexham, Mold & Connah's Quay Ry* [1899] 1 Ch. 440.

[18] There is some argument whether this lender's right is strictly subrogation at all, or a separate species of equitable claim; but the distinction does not seem to be an important one.

[19] E.g. *The Tagus* [1903] P 44.

[20] Insolvency Act 1986, Schedule 6, §11.

[21] [1902] 1 Ch. 1; on appeal [1903] A.C. 6.

[22] *Brocklesby v. Temperance Permanent Building Society* [1895] A.C. 173 (mortgage entered into without authority of borrower).

security: he must have been obliged to do so[23] under his agreement with the lender. Secondly, there is authority that if the security taken by the lender is valid at the outset but is later invalidated, subrogation will not be allowed: the previous security paid off is regarded as abandoned by the taking of a new valid security, and cannot later be revived even if the later security is successfully impugned. Thus a person taking from a company a charge which is provisionally valid, but which fails to be registered under the Companies Act 1985[24] and ultimately fails for non-registration, cannot rely on subrogation[25]. Although the question has not yet arisen for decision, a similar rule could well apply where the security taken by the lender is later impugned for undue influence: as with the company cases, the taking of the initially valid security may very well be regarded as extinguishing permanently any unpaid vendor's lien or other security[26].

3   SURETIES, ETC.

We have seen[27] that a surety can sue the principal debtor for **12-08** recoupment. But this is only a personal claim: parallel to it, the surety also has the right on payment to stand in the shoes of the creditor and enforce any remedies the latter may have had against the debtor. This is important for two reasons. The creditor may have taken security, in which case the surety can himself become a secured creditor of the original debtor[28]; equally, the creditor may be a preferred creditor in the debtor's insolvency[29] (though with the reduction in the numbers of secured creditors since the Insolvency Act 1986 this latter category is not as important as it once was[30]).

This right, which can only be exercised after full payment, and then only for the amount actually paid by the surety (e.g. if he settled the debt for less than its face value), applies to all securities, whenever taken, and whether or not the surety knew about them[31] - causing occasionally, it

---

[23] See *Wylie v. Carlyon* [1922] 1 Ch. 51; *Orakpo v. Manson Investments* [1977] 3 All E.R. 1, 7 (Lord Diplock).

[24] I.e. s. 395 ff.

[25] *Burston Finance v. Speirway* [1974] 3 All E.R. 735.

[26] Hence perhaps explaining why subrogation was not claimed in *National Westminster Bank v. Morgan* [1985] A.C. 686.

[27] Para. 12-05 above.

[28] *Morgan v. Seymour* (1638) 1 Ch. R. 120.

[29] E.g. *Re Lamplugh Iron Ore Co.* [1927] 1 Ch. 308; *Re Downer Enterprises* [1974] 2 All E.R. 1074.

[30] But one case which would still succeed under this head is *Re Downer Enterprises* [1974] 2 All E.R. 1074.

[31] See *Mayhew v. Crickett* (1818) 2 Swan 185, 191; *cf Duncan Fox v. North & South Wales Bank* (1879) 6 App. Cas. 1.

must be said, a windfall for the surety concerned. Nor does it matter that the right which the surety seeks to take over was technically extinguished by his payment to the creditor: securities are deemed to be kept alive in equity, and statute[32] has intervened to prevent the debtor taking advantage of the old common–law rule that debts owed by him jointly with the surety were *ipso facto* extinguished by payment on the part of the surety.

A similar right is given to those who are not technically sureties but are regarded as analogous: for instance, indorsers of bills of exchange[33], who are in effect sureties for the acceptor, and original lessees, who remain liable for rent that ought really to be paid for the assignee[34].

4 SUBROGATION AND INSURANCE

12-09   It is a feature of an indemnity insurance contract that the assured ought not to recover more than he has lost: in so far as he does, he is regarded as unjustly enriched *vis-à-vis* the underwriter who bore the risk. Although sometimes treated as a self-evident[35] and independent head of unjust enrichment, the basis of this doctrine is essentially contractual[36]; it arises from the nature of the contract between insured and underwriter. Sometimes indeed the underwriter gets his remedy without any need to invoke subrogation in the sense of a transfer of an obligation. Suppose I sell my car to you on the basis that risk passes immediately but property only next week; it then becomes a total loss in the intervening period and I claim on my insurance. If you subsequently pay me the price (as you are bound to) I must account to the insurers, since otherwise I would be paid twice for the same loss[37]. Nevertheless, the commonest way in which the underwriter obtains his remedy is by subrogation proper, i.e. where the insured, having been paid for a loss by his insurer, has a claim against a third

---

[32] Mercantile Law Amendment Act 1856, s. 5.

[33] The indorser has a right by statute (Bills of Exchange Act 1882, s. 59(2)(b)) to sue the acceptor: but this has been extended to give him a right to any securities held by the acceptor: *Duncan Fox v. North & South Wales Bank* (1880) 6 App. Cas. 1.

[34] *Re Downer Enterprises* [1974] 2 All E.R. 1074.

[35] Which of course it is not. It is perfectly arguable that, if I choose to pay to insure my property, any recovery from my underwriters has been paid for by me and I should be allowed to keep it in addition to any other recovery I am lucky enough to get from third parties. *Cf* the treatment of collateral benefits in cases of tort recovery for personal injury: *Parry v. Cleaver* [1970] A.C. 1.

[36] See *Yorkshire Insurance v. Nisbet Shipping* [1962] 2 Q.B. 330, 339-340. But *cf Lucas v. E.C.G.D.* [1973] 2 All E.R. 984.

[37] *Castellain v. Preston* (1883) 11 Q.B.D. 380. Not so with payments that do not go to reduce the loss, however: *cf Burnand v. Rodocanachi* (1882) 7 App. Cas. 333.

party in respect of that claim. In this situation the underwriter is entitled to take over the insured's claim and exercise it for his own benefit[38].

The underwriter's interest in any right of recovery depends on the circumstances (and on the terms of the contract of insurance). It cannot normally exceed the amount he has paid out[39], even in the case of a valued policy. In the event of under-insurance it seems that the assured takes priority over the underwriter in any recovery until, coupled with anything recovered from the underwriter, he has been fully indemnified[40]: on the other hand, where there is an 'excess' clause the assured is to that extent subordinated to the underwriter until the latter is fully indemnified[41].

12-10

---

[38] *Quaere* whether the assured holds his right of action on trust for the underwriter, or whether the latter has merely a lien over it. The point was left open by the House of Lords in *Lord Napier & Ettrick v. Hunter* [1993] 1 All E.R. 385.

[39] But no further: *Yorkshire Insurance Co. v. Nisbet Shipping* [1962] 2 Q.B. 330. (Unless, of course, the contract so provides: *Lucas v. E.C.G.D.* [1973] 2 All E.R. 984.)

[40] *Confederation Life Ins Co. v. Causton* (1989) 60 D.L.R. (4th) 372, 374; *Lord Napier & Ettrick v. Hunter* [1993] 1 All E.R. 385, 390.

[41] *Lord Napier & Ettrick v. Hunter* [1993] 1 All E.R. 385.

CHAPTER 13

RESTITUTION AND PUBLIC AUTHORITIES

As with contract and tort, so with restitution; public authorities, not **13–01** to mention others subject to public law statutory duties[1], are *prima facie* subject to the same restitutionary rights and duties as anyone else. However, restitutionary claims by and against such authorities have, in practice, to be subject to qualifications and exceptions; one cannot treat government in its various forms simply as if it were a species of private citizen or company[2]. It is the special rules applicable to public authorities that this chapter deals with, and in particular three points.

The first point is the predominant place given to statute. In the nature **13–02** of things a large proportion of public bodies' income takes the form of taxes and statutory charges, while a good deal of their expenditure consists of statutory grants and benefits payable to private citizens or other public organisations. And the problems of overpaid (or underestimated) tax and benefits are largely dealt with by statute rather than by common law or equitable principles. The second issue is that, because public authority is at times expected to play fairer than private enterprise[3], the grounds for restitution against it may exceptionally be wider than those elsewhere. The common law action for recovery of tax overpaid (in the rare cases where it lies), and the principle known as extortion *colore officii*, both dealt with below, are examples of this.

The third point is that public authorities may have certain advantages not shared by other litigants, in terms of specific defences available to them or not available to those in conflict with them. Limitations on the right to recover overpaid taxes, and on the extent to which a public authority can be estopped, are good examples.

---

[1]   E.g. electricity, gas and water utilities.
[2]   See the comments of La Forest J in *Air Canada v. British Columbia* [1989] 1 S.C.R. 1133, 1201.
[3]   *Cf* the 'officers of the court' exception in the case of money paid under a mistake of law: *Ex. p. James* (1874) L.R. 9 Ch. App. 609.

1 STATUTE

13-03   Specific provisions cover overpaid taxes[4], business rates[5], council tax[6] and VAT[7]. Although they vary, a common feature is that there is no specific requirement of mistake, duress or some other feature that would be necessary in an action between private persons: subject to a number of specific defences, all that has to be shown is that tax has been paid that was not properly exigible, thus getting close to a general *conditio indebiti*, or legal principle that payments of money not owed are *prima facie* recoverable[8]. A similar principle applies to overpaid social security benefit[9].

A further important feature of the statutory schemes is that sometimes the right of the taxpayer to reimbursement is not absolute, but qualified by a reference to reasonableness[10] or conditional on some over-riding discretion given by statute to the public authority concerned. To some extent this negatives the idea of any 'right' to repayment existing at all. On the other hand, this difference is not as important as it might seem. Such statutory discretions, whether to seek or to withhold repayment, are on principle subject to judicial review: and in *Tower Hamlets Borough Council v. Chetnik Developments*[11], where a local authority's discretion to refund overpaid rates was in issue, the House of Lords explicitly relied on analogies from the private law of restitution in striking down the authority's decision to refuse a refund[12].

2 PARTICULAR PUBLIC LAW RIGHTS TO RESTITUTION

Payments *colore officii*

13-04   In many cases public authorities are bound to do things, such as providing services, issuing licences, and so on, either for no charge or for

---

[4]   Taxes Management Act 1970, s. 33.

[5]   See S.I. 1989/1058, §22.

[6]   See S.I. 1992/613, §24.

[7]   Finance Act 1989, s. 24.

[8]   Which does not, of course, exist as a general rule: see *Woolwich Building Society v. IRC (No. 2)* [1992] 3 All E.R. 737, 759 (Lord Goff).

[9]   Social Security Administration Act 1992, s. 71.

[10]   As in s. 33 of the Taxes Management Act 1970, for example.

[11]   [1988] 1 All E.R. 961.

[12]   But in the case of rates the discretion to repay has now been replaced by a right to reimbursement: S.I. 1989/1058, §22.

a limited fee. There is no doubt that a decision by an authority to demand a fee for what it is bound to provide for nothing, or ask for a larger fee than that allowed, is susceptible to judicial review[13]; but what if the fee is paid and then demanded back? The answer is that *prima facie* recovery is allowed; see, for instance, *Morgan v. Palmer*[14], where the plaintiff successfully recovered a sum paid for a licence which the defendant had no authority to charge. A similar principle applies to non-public bodies, such as utilities, which are charged with specific statutory duties to provide services at particular prices[15].

It might be argued that these are really cases of duress. If I pay you £100 to avert a threat by you to break your contract, I can recover it[16]; is it not the same if I pay you £100 to do something you are bound to do by statute rather than contract? However, while the principles are the same, the recovery is rather wider in the latter case. Not only is it arguable that I do not have to show a positive threat by you not to perform your duty[17]; more importantly, in most cases of non-performance of a public duty my only recourse is to an application for judicial review[18], and hence it is unlikely that there would be a sufficient wrongful act (in the sense of something for which you could be sued for damages) to found a claim based on duress proper.

Taxes

In the rare case where statute does not regulate recovery, overpaid taxes create problems for traditional restitution law. The difficulty is twofold. First, while some overpayments are covered by traditional restitution concepts (e.g. where I miscompute my income, and thus pay under a mistake of fact), many are not: either the mistake will be one of law[19], or there will be a genuine dispute with the taxing authorities as to what is exigible. In either case there is no traditional peg on which to hang a claim for recompense.

13-05

---

13 E.g. *R v. Richmond-on-Thames B.C. ex. p. McCarthy & Stone* [1991] 4 All E.R. 897 (unlawful charge for preliminary consultations on planning applications).

14 (1824) 2 B & C 729. See too *Steele v. Williams* (1853) 8 Ex. 625; *Hooper v. Exeter Corp.* (1887) 56 L.J.Q.B. 457, and the discussion of the whole matter in *Woolwich Building Society v. IRC (No. 2)* [1992] 3 All E.R. 737.

15 E.g. *G.W.R. v. Sutton* (1869) L.R. 4 H.L. 226 (railway); *South of Scotland Electricity Board v. B.O.C.* [1959] 2 All E.R. 225 (electricity supplier).

16 See Chapter 4 above.

17 None seems to have been apparent in, e.g. *Hooper v. Exeter Corp.* (1887) 56 L.J.Q.B. 457. *Twyford v. Manchester Corp.* [1946] Ch. 236, apparently holding the opposite, was doubted by Glidewell LJ in the Court of Appeal in the *Woolwich* case: [1991] 4 All E.R. 577, 601.

18 Because of the principle in *O'Reilly v. Mackman* [1983] 2 A.C. 237.

19 On which see para. 3-23 ff, above.

Secondly, many tax payments – at least those which are clearly disputed – are made against the background of an overt or implicit threat of legal proceedings; and in general a claimant who chooses to pay in response to a legal demand rather than take the risk of disputing it in court will lose any right to impugn it later.

13-06 Nevertheless, in *Woolwich Building Society v. IRC (No. 2)*[20], a case where the plaintiff society had overpaid some £50m in tax but relevant statutory provisions did not apply[21], the House of Lords by a bare majority overcame both these problems. The lack of any traditional head of restitution was countered by reference to constitutional principle in the shape of the prohibition in the Bill of Rights 1688[22] against the levying of taxes not authorised by Parliament: this, coupled with a judgment that public authorities were in a peculiarly powerful position *vis-à-vis* the taxpayer, and ought to be under particular duties of probity, was held sufficient to create a specific head of recovery. As for the point of payment against a threat of litigation, this again fell victim to the principle that the state should be distinguished from other claimants; while any other citizen who threatened litigation in good faith could reasonably expect to keep the fruits of his endeavour, however unwilling the payer, the overwhelming power of the state dictated that it should not share this privilege. Only in the event of a truly voluntary intent on the part of the taxpayer to pay to close the transaction would recovery be barred.

Recovery by the Crown of unauthorised payments

13-07 On the basis of the constitutional maxim that any expenditure by the Crown must be sanctioned by Parliament, it has long been held that any payment by the Crown specifically found to be unauthorised is *ipso facto* recoverable from the recipient as money had and received[23] (and probably by way of equitable proprietary claim in so far as the recipient, or any subsequent person other than a bona fide purchaser, still has it). This principle clearly has affinities with that covering reimbursement of *ultra vires* payments generally; it is not entirely clear whether it is in fact the same. In particular, while actions to recoup *ultra vires* payments are clearly subject to general restitutionary defences such as change of

---

[20] [1992] 3 All E.R. 737. Although the Revenue later returned the sum involved, the case was litigated over the claimants' desire for interest on the sums concerned while in the Revenue's hands (totalling nearly £8 million). If the claimants had no right to recovery, interest was not payable; if they had such a right, it was.

[21] Because the tax concerned had been demanded under the provisions of a void statutory instrument, the relevant provisions did not cover it.

[22] Article 4.

[23] *Auckland Harbour Board v. R* [1924] A.C. 318 is the classic authority.

position[24], there is also authority that actions by the Crown in this connection are not[25]. It remains to be seen whether they will in due course be assimilated to the general rule.

3 RESTRICTIONS ON RECOVERY AGAINST PUBLIC AUTHORITIES

Procedural

Restitutionary claims against public authorities based on overpaid tax or on the invalidity of a demand may face one of two extra procedural hurdles.   **13-08**

The first concerns the place of judicial review. Under the rule in *O'Reilly v. Mackman*[26], a person wishing to challenge the exercise of a public law power must in general do so by way of judicial review under R.S.C., Order 53 rather than by a private law action; it is therefore arguable that an action seeking to recover an overpayment without first seeking judicial review will be struck out as an abuse of process[27]. If so this may be highly important. Not only is judicial review, unlike restitutionary recovery, a discretionary remedy; it is also subject to a very short time limit. However, the point is by no means clear. There is authority that the rule in *O'Reilly v. Mackman*[28] does not apply to a case where private law rights are in issue, at least where these 'dominate' the proceedings[29]; and it may well be that this exception would apply so as to allow actions to be brought directly for the repayment of tax or for restitution of payments made *colore officii* without the necessity of a prior challenge by way of application for judicial review[30].   **13-09**

The second problem concerns rights of appeal. In most cases of tax[31], and in many concerning other charges by public authorities, a statutory right of appeal against a charge is given. Does the existence of such a right

---

24 *Westdeutsche Landesbank Girozentrale v. London Borough of Islington, The Times*, 23 February 1993.

25 *Cf Commonwealth v. Burns* [1971] V.R. 825.

26 [1983] 2 A.C. 237.

27 In the *Woolwich Building Society* case itself the taxpayers, before suing to recover the excess, first brought judicial review proceedings (see [1991] 4 All E.R. 92) to establish that the demand was unlawful. It followed that no *O'Reilly v. Mackman* point could conceivably be taken.

28 [1983] 2 A.C. 237.

29 See in particular *Roy v. Kensington FPC* [1992] 1 All E.R. 705, 729.

30 If so, did the Woolwich Building Society waste its money (and the taxpayer's) in bringing its original proceedings for judicial review?

31 Though not on the special facts of the *Woolwich* case, where no such right existed.

preclude restitutionary proceedings in the ordinary courts? Glidewell LJ in the *Woolwich* case in the Court of Appeal[32] left the point open; but on principle it is submitted that it must have this effect, at least where the statute provides machinery for repayment. It is a general rule that statutory rights of challenge preclude private law actions[33]; and there is no reason to treat actions based on unjustified enrichment any differently. Furthermore, even if the right of appeal does not oust restitution proceedings entirely, it is suggested that failure to exercise it before bringing those proceedings may give cause for striking out as an abuse of process, or at least for penalisation in costs[34].

Substantive – change of position

13-10   Since *Westdeutsche Landesbank v. London Borough of Islington*[35], it is clear that the defence of change of position is available to public authorities as to anyone else. On the other hand, in the nature of things its ambit of the defence is likely to be rather different. The idea of central government being able to show a change of position resulting from a belief in the security of a given tax receipt from a particular person is, to say the least, far-fetched. On the other hand, it is a good deal more plausible that local government may well be able to show that, by budgeting for a given receipt, it has changed its position[36]: indeed, it may be able to raise the defence in a number of situations where it would not be available to a private litigant – e.g. if it could show that it has lost the right to raise taxation in a subsequent year, or has lost the opportunity to claim some grant or rebate from another source[37].

There is, however, another problem. Suppose a local authority charges large numbers of ratepayers with an *ultra vires* business rate or other tax, in reliance on which it incurs additional irrecoverable expenditure; later, one taxpayer sues to recover what he has paid. Can the authority show change of position? Taken in aggregate, it clearly can; as against the individual claimant, it will probably be unable to. Presumably the change of position defence will be flexible enough to take account of this problem and, where necessary, allow reduction *pro rata* of claims.

---

[32] [1991] 4 All E.R. 577, 602.

[33] See e.g. *Calveley v. Merseyside Chief Constable* [1989] 1 All E.R. 1025 (statutory right of appeal precludes negligence proceedings).

[34] *Cf Roy v. Kensington FPC* [1992] 1 All E.R. 705, 715, *per* Lord Lowry.

[35] *The Times*, 23 February 1993.

[36] Or where a local authority has paid over rating receipts to another authority under 'precepting' provisions: *Spiers & Pond v. Finsbury MBC* (1956) 1 Ryde's R.C. 219 (*semble*).

[37] Argued, unsuccessfully on the facts, by Islington Council in *Westdeutsche Landesbank v. London Borough of Islington, The Times*, 23 February 1993.

Substantive – unjust enrichment of the plaintiff if recovery is allowed

On occasion, taxes or other charges payable to public authorities are **13-11** recoverable by the taxpayer from third parties: VAT is a classic example. It follows that if recovery is allowed against the authority, the claimant may effectively gets a windfall. In *Woolwich Building Society v. IRC (No. 2)*[38] Lord Goff left the point open whether this would provide a defence to the authority concerned. Although the provision of a defence along these lines is superficially attractive, however, it is tentatively suggested that recovery should be allowed even here. First, it is quite possible that the third party from whom the tax was recoverable would himself have a right to restitution[39] against the taxpayer, at least where the latter got his payment back from the authority[40]: if so, justice would be done all round. And in any case it is not immediately apparent why the taxing authority should itself be entitled to a windfall arising from arrangements between the taxpayer and third parties[41].

---

[38] [1992] 3 All E.R. 737, 764. *Cf* the Canadian decision in *Air Canada v. British Columbia* (1989) 59 D.L.R. (4th) 161.

[39] E.g. for money paid by mistake.

[40] If he did not, presumably he would have a defence of change of position.

[41] *Cf* the position in the law of damages. A plaintiff has a right to recover his loss from a wrongdoer, and it is *nil ad rem* that arrangements between himself and a third party meant he did not in fact pay for it out of his own pocket: see, e.g. *Jones v. Stroud DC* [1988] 1 All E.R. 5, and *Linden Gardens v. Lenesta* [1993] 3 All E.R. 417.

CHAPTER 14

OFFICIOUSNESS AND FORCED EXCHANGE

1 LACK OF FREE ACCEPTANCE: THE PRINCIPLE AGAINST FORCED EXCHANGE

There are two sides to free acceptance in restitution law. We have **14-01** seen it so far[1] as a creator of rights: acceptance of a benefit, at least when accompanied by an understanding that it is to be paid for, is itself a ground of restitutionary recovery. This chapter deals with the converse of this proposition, which can be christened the principle against forced exchange. Under this, even if there are *prima facie* grounds for restitution, such as mistake, the fact that the defendant had no chance to accept or reject the benefit concerned will - particularly in the case of services rendered - act as a *prima facie* bar to recovery. Faced with the choice of forcing an exchange on an unwilling defendant and short-changing a possibly deserving plaintiff, the law's understandable reaction is to follow the lead of the law of contract[2] and choose the latter.

We have already come across this phenomenon in connection with **14-02** mistake, where (unless and until overruled) the decision in *Falcke v. Scottish Imperial Assurance Co.*[3] seems to bar any action for services rendered in error, however clear the benefit actually gained by the defendant. Similarly too (outside specialised contexts such as medical services and maritime salvage) with necessitous intervention; and also with partial performance rendered by a contract-breaker[4].

Having said this, two issues need looking at more closely. First, what amounts to lack of free acceptance for these purposes? Secondly - and vastly more importantly - when will the law, exceptionally, relax the requirement that there be an acceptance at all?

---

[1] See Chapter 5 above.

[2] I.e. the rule in *Felthouse v. Bindley* (1862) 11 C.B.N.S. 869, that a bargain cannot be pushed on an unwilling contractor and then cemented by his silence.

[3] (1886) 34 Ch. D. 234. It is true that the case is hardly strong authority. The plaintiff failed to establish his mistake on the facts: the defendant had no chance to reject the benefit: and the plaintiff was claiming, not recompense, but a lien on the policy. But there are still strong *dicta* against recovery even as a matter of principle.

[4] *Miles v. Wakefield M.B.C.* [1987] 1 All E.R. 1089. See too para. 6-08 above.

2 DEFINITION OF FREE ACCEPTANCE

14-03   What amounts to lack of free acceptance in this context? The extreme case is easy: if it is literally impossible for you to avoid being benefited, then obviously there is no free acceptance – indeed, there is no acceptance at all. You clean my windows by mistake: I cannot unclean them. Or take the facts of *Owen v. Tate*[5]. A owed his bank £350, secured by title deeds owned by B. C undertook to pay the bank what was owing, and later, on demand from the bank, paid it; despite A's protests the bank released the title deeds to B. C sued A for restitution, and not surprisingly failed; even if C had a *prima facie* right to restitution, A had had no ability whatever to prevent his overdraft being cleared and the title deeds released[6].

The more important question is: assuming the defendant had some choice in the matter, when will his acceptance be 'free'? The answer seems to be: only if (a) his acceptance was unconditional and properly informed; and (b) he could reasonably have been expected to exercise some choice in the matter. This is a restrictive answer, as indeed it should be: it is only in the plainest case that an exchange of any sort should be forced on an unwilling defendant.

Unconditionality: lack of proper information

14-04   The classic case of conditional acceptance has been dealt with elsewhere: that is, the contractor who breaks his contract having partly performed. In a sense the other party to the contract has willingly received the benefits he got: nevertheless this is not a case of free acceptance, since he only willingly received it on the (unfulfilled) basis that it would in time mature into full performance. Hence he does not have to pay for what he got, unless some separate act amounting to acceptance can be shown[7].

On the question of lack of proper information, suppose a practical joker telephones you in my name and agrees to pay you £10 to dig my garden; he then tells me that you intend to do the job as a favour to me, whereupon I allow you to do it. I have in a sense accepted your services mistakenly rendered; nevertheless I should not be liable to pay for them.

---

[5]   [1985] 2 All E.R. 129.

[6]   It seems to have been accepted that C's payment, C being a guarantor, discharged A. For criticism see generally Beatson, *The Use and Abuse of Unjust Enrichment*, Chapter 7.

[7]   On which see *Wiluszynski v. Tower Hamlets L.B.C.* [1989] I.R.L.R. 259, below.

Boulton v. Jones[8], already discussed in the context of liability based on free acceptance, is a neat example of this problem; although Boulton arguably supplied the piping to Jones under a mistake[9], there should be no restitutionary recovery since Jones did not accept it with full information as to the true state of affairs.

One case gives particular difficulty in this context. In *Upton-on Severn RDC v. Powell*[10] the defendant saw a fire in his barn. He telephoned the police; the police called in the Upton fire brigade, who came and put it out. Unfortunately no-one realised that the defendant lived outside the area where he was entitled to the services of the brigade free of charge. The local authority successfully sued for services rendered. The ground on which the action succeeded was that the defendant had contracted for the brigade's services; but this is highly doubtful, and it has been suggested that this case is better regarded as one of restitutionary recovery. It is respectfully submitted, however, that this cannot be right. Even if the defendant accepted the services, he did so under a misapprehension and therefore did not accept them freely. It follows, it is suggested, that unless it can be supported on contractual grounds, the *Upton-on-Severn case* should be regarded as wrongly decided.

Reasonable opportunity to reject

A person will not be deemed to have freely accepted something   **14-05**
where his choice in the matter was, as a matter of practical and commercial reality, constrained. In *Wiluszynski v. Tower Hamlets L.B.C.*[11] council employees wrongfully refused, as part of industrial action, to answer enquiries from councillors, but otherwise worked normally. The Council told them this was unacceptable, but took no steps to dismiss them or prevent them from doing the work they were willing to do. They were held not liable to pay anything for the work actually done: the mere fact that they had not locked out the workers concerned did not mean they had 'freely' accepted the work they did perform.

---

8 (1857) 2 H & N 564.
9 I.e. he thought, wrongly, that there was a valid contract between them.
10 [1942] 1 All E.R. 220.
11 [1989] I.R.L.R. 259.

3 EXCEPTIONS TO THE REQUIREMENT OF FREE ACCEPTANCE

14-06   We now turn to the second question: how far should the courts be prepared to relax the requirement of free acceptance and make a defendant pay for something he never asked for and could not avoid benefiting from?

Benefits rendered under compulsion

14-07   One case is well established: if my ground for restitution against you is based on compulsion[12], then whether you had a chance to reject that benefit is irrelevant. Take the assignor of a lease sued for rent owing by the assignee: having paid, he can sue the assignee for recoupment quite independently of whether the latter consented to having his debt discharged. The reason is not hard to seek: the two compulsions, so to speak, cancel each other out and disentitle the defendant from arguing that he should not have to pay for something he did not want in the first place.

14-08   Note, however, that the question of what sort of compulsion acting on the plaintiff will defeat a plea of 'no free acceptance' is answered pragmatically. Mere formal liability to be sued will not, without more, suffice. Go back to the facts of *Owen v. Tate*[13]; there, the plaintiff, before paying off the defendant's overdraft, had made himself technically liable to do so by guaranteeing it. The Court of Appeal held that this made no difference; it was admitted that the undertaking was entirely voluntary, and in deciding whether a plaintiff had been forced to discharge an obligation, the circumstances of its acceptance were as much in account as those of its discharge.

If so, however, this raises a further difficulty. Most people forced to discharge another's liability (or confer some other benefit on him) originally acted voluntarily, at least to some degree. I do not have to become a lessee at all, still less having done so to assign my lease to you so as to put myself at risk of having to pay your rent. I do not have to leave my chattels on your leasehold property so as to make them liable to distress for your rent[14]. Yet in both cases I have a restitutionary claim against you if I am made to discharge your obligation. Why? The suggestion in *Owen v. Tate*[15] is that it all depends on whether I am

---

12   Note the need for compulsion, not mere involuntariness due to e.g. mistake.
13   [1985] 2 All E.R. 129.
14   As in *Exall v. Partridge* (1799) 8 T.R. 308.
15   [1985] 2 All E.R. 129.

'officious'; if I am I fail, whereas if I act (for instance) under 'necessity', then the result may be different. But this is not entirely satisfactory. The law has - quite rightly, it is suggested - set its face against rewarding the necessitous intervener as such: why privilege the intervener whose action took the form of undertaking a liability to a third party? It would be odd indeed if your neighbour who spent money repairing your roof after a gale recovered nothing, whereas your other neighbour who guaranteed your mortgage payments while you were away and then paid them recovered in full.

With respect, it is suggested that a better criterion is a broader one: did the claimant undertake liability for the defendant's debt for good business reasons independently of any effect on the defendant, or did he do so with a view to helping the defendant? In the former case he should recover[16]; in the latter, he should not.

Incontrovertible benefit: a doubtful concept

We have argued so far, and will continue to argue, that the soundest justification for the 'no free acceptance' rule is the presumption against forced exchange. Restitution, while independent of contract, cannot be allowed to act without regard to it; and just as the law of contract will not make you pay for goods or services in the absence of clear evidence that you agreed to buy them, the law of restitution should be equally circumspect in making you pay unless there is clear evidence that you assented to get them. This is, as has been mentioned, the assumption lying behind cases such as *Falcke v. Scottish Imperial Assurance Co.*[17].

14-09

A competing justification is, however, possible. On this argument, the reason why we do not generally force people to pay for what they have not accepted is not consent-based but economic: it is that goods and services are only worth what the recipient is prepared to pay for them, and there is normally no evidence that the involuntary recipient of largesse would have wanted to pay for it at all (the phenomenon referred to by Professor Birks as 'subjective devaluation'[18]).

The significance of this is not hard to spot. Imagine - exceptionally - that the recipient (a) did not in fact consent; but (b) would in fact have obtained and paid for the benefit even if the plaintiff had not rendered it (or, *a fortiori*, that since its receipt he has since turned it into money): assume, in other words, that he has obtained an 'incontrovertible

14-10

---

[16] As in e.g. *The Zuhal K* [1987] 1 Lloyds Rep. 1.

[17] (1886) 34 Ch. D. 234. But see the comments on this case at para. 8-02 above. Nevertheless, there are still strong *dicta* against recovery, even as a matter of principle.

[18] Birks, *An Introduction to the Law of Restitution*, pp.109 ff.

benefit'[19]. On this argument – contrary to the 'forced exchange' principle – there is nothing wrong in forcing him to pay. Take some obvious instances. Suppose I paint your house by mistake while you are away[20]: suppose I can also show that on your return you would have had it painted anyway. Is it unjust to make you pay me rather than your usual painter? Again, suppose I repair your house after storm damage, whereupon you immediately put it on the market and sell it at an increased price: is there any reason why I should not claim the profit from you? Yet again, imagine the plaintiff is prepared to waive any right to recompense unless and until the benefit is encashed by the defendant. Take the facts of *Falcke*. Grant that the policy owner should not be made to reimburse the payer immediately from money he may not have: but is it equally wrong to give the payer a lien over the policy, such that if the owner were to cash it in the payer would have first claim on the proceeds?

14-11   This thinking is at first sight attractive. It is nevertheless tentatively suggested that it is flawed, and that (despite considerable academic, and on occasion judicial[21], support for the concept of 'incontrovertible benefit', recovery remains misconceived even in these cases.

To begin with, it is (it is suggested) contrary to the whole basis of the law of obligations to adjust obligations on the basis of hypothetical, rather than real, desires. If I steal your Rembrandt, you can sue me for its value; it makes no difference to my liability that you did not really want it[22], or (it is suggested) that you would have given it to me had I asked. Again, I cannot impose a contract on you to buy my car by saying I will assume your silence amounts to acceptance; and it makes no difference whatever that you would have had to buy a car anyway, or even that you would, if you had had pencil and paper to hand, have accepted my offer. What matters is actual assent: and the same should, it is suggested, be true of restitution.

The second objection is that, effectively if not ostensibly, it subjects the defendant to a test of 'reasonableness' in the management of his affairs. For the defendant's own decision whether he wanted the benefit concerned, is substituted the court's decision on whether he could reasonably be thought to be worse off if he were forced to pay for it. This may be acceptable where the law itself compels the plaintiff to benefit the defendant; having forced a transfer one way, it can hardly do less than compel due restitution the other. But in other cases, it is suggested, the

---

[19]   The phrase is Professor Jones's, and is the other side of the 'subjective devaluation' coin.

[20]   Not entirely far-fetched: I could have agreed to paint your neighbour's house and then mistaken the premises.

[21]   E.g. *The Manila* [1988] 3 All E.R. 843, 855 (Hirst J).

[22]   *Cf The Mediana* [1900] A.C. 113, 117 (Lord Halsbury).

'incontrovertible benefit' principle takes the function of the court as adjuster of rights far too far. The citizen's right not to be affected in the management of his property without his consent is an important right, and one for the exercise of which he ought not for that reason to be accountable: he should be able to exercise it, and to decline to accept any benefit, for any reason, good or bad, or indeed for no reason. It is not the function of the state to interfere with this action, however selfish, unreasonable or capricious it may be.

CHAPTER 15

DEFENCES

Where specifically relevant, details of the defences to given **15-01**
restitution claims have already been dealt with in the chapters relating to
those claims. This chapter aims to provide a more general overall view of
the subject.

1 EXCLUSION OF RESTITUTION BY AGREEMENT
AND SIMILAR CASES

By contract or compromise

Restitutionary rights, like any others, may be excluded by contract **15-02**
inter partes. Assume I order goods from you, sending a deposit which is
agreed to be non-refundable in any event, even if you are in breach of
contract. Or again, assume I have a running account with you subject to
an agreement that no claim will lie for inadvertent overpayment unless
made within 48 hours. Such exclusions of restitutionary rights are
perfectly valid at common law[1]. Similarly with *bona fide* compromises –
which are, after all, merely a species of contract, but which frequently in
practice affect restitutionary claims. If you demand £1,000 from me by
threatening to commit what is in fact a breach of contract (though you in
good faith think it is not), whereupon I pay you £500 to end the
dispute, I recover nothing. I cannot go back on our agreement to
compromise the matter.

Finality: intent to close a transaction

There are many cases of payments or other benefits held to give rise **15-03**
to no right of recovery on the basis that they are 'once-and-for-all',
which nevertheless cannot be explained as compromises. An agreement to
compromise is only effective as such if there is indeed a genuine dispute

---

[1]   Indeed, they are probably not covered by the Unfair Contract Terms Act 1977 either.
Section 3 of that Act only covers exclusions of one's duty to perform one's contract; whereas
restitutionary liability arises extra-contractually.

to compose[2], and if the person seeking to rely on it was acting in good faith in giving up his supposed rights[3]: if either of these factors is lacking there is no consideration for the agreement. Nevertheless, even here there is no reason in principle why a person should not waive his restitutionary rights. Suppose I give you £100 as a reward for passing the Bar exams, but say it will not worry me if in fact you have not. Again, imagine you contract to do work on my house, but later, in full knowledge that you have no right to do so, refuse to perform unless I pay you a further £250 to cover increased costs. Feeling sympathetic, and in order to cement our business relationship, I do so; I cannot recover my payment[4].

Donative intent

15-04   For obvious reasons, benefits rendered with the intent of making a gift of them cannot form the subject of restitutionary recovery; English law does not generally allow people, however deserving, to repent of largesse.

In many cases, indeed, absence of donative intent does not need to be specifically mentioned since it is implicit in the requirements for restitution to be granted in the first place. Free acceptance, for instance, means free acceptance on the basis that what was accepted was to be paid for. If you freely accept goods or services which I offer to you gratis, my claim to be paid for them simply cannot get off the ground. Again, the right of a would-be contractor to recover for services rendered in the expectation that a contract would later materialise is well established; but it only applies where there is no understanding that the services are to be rendered without payment (for example as a 'loss leader', in order to encourage the recipient to do business in future).

15-05   Nevertheless, in other cases donative intent does provide an independent defence to a restitutionary claim that would otherwise exist. Take a typical duress case, as where a robber threatens to stab me unless I give him my purse. It is possible, if unlikely, that I will genuinely decide that I wish to give it to him out of sympathy for his plight. If I do, I cannot later get it back[5]. Or imagine necessity; if I am your agent of necessity or someone else who would otherwise have a claim against you for

---

[2]   E.g. *Sneath v. Valley Gold* [1893] 1 Q.B. 477; D. Foskett, *The Law and Practice of Compromise,* 3rd ed., §2-01.

[3]   See *Callisher v. Bischoffsheim* (1870) L.R. 5 Q.B. 449, 451.

[4]   *Cf Williams v. Roffey Bros.* [1990] 1 All E.R. 512. It is inconceivable that the court would have allowed restitution of the extra payment if it had been made.

[5]   *Cf The Siboen & The Sibotre* [1976] 1 Lloyds Rep. 293 (a case of duress by threatened breach of contract).

necessitous intervention, but act purely out of motives of friendship or otherwise make it clear that I will not charge for my services, it is submitted that that is an end of the matter: I cannot later change my mind[6].

Presumably in all these cases what matters is not so much the claimant's actual state of mind, but the outward manifestation of it: if a reasonable person would have thought he was acting *gratis*, then that should have been sufficient[7].

2 BONA FIDE PURCHASE AND DISCHARGE OF OBLIGATIONS

Bona fide purchase

This is not a full-blown defence in its own right, but rather an inherent limitation on certain sorts of restitutionary claim: in particular, claims – such as 'tracing' claims – lying against a particular thing or fund, rather than simply for a money payment. Its main effects appear below. **15-06**

First, assuming a transfer of personal chattels is voidable for fraud, or mistake[8], it remains so voidable as against anyone who has the chattels concerned at the time. But this does not apply to a bona fide purchaser; once he has obtained rights in the chattel, those are indefeasible.

Secondly, the right to trace in equity – whether affecting the plaintiff's actual property or its proceeds – and indeed any claim based on a constructive trust, equally stops as soon as those proceeds have reached the hands of a bona fide purchaser.

Thirdly, as mentioned in Chapter 10, bona fide purchase for value stops so-called 'common law tracing'. At common law if you receive – however innocently – money representing[9] property stolen from me, you become liable to an action for money had and received; but this does not apply where you took the money in good faith and for value. (Note, however, that this formulation of the rule is limited to recipients of *money*. In the absence of a right to trace in equity, the recipient of any

---

6 Compare the rendering of emergency medical attention in England: arguably the most convincing reason for denying a claim against the victim is the universal acceptance that such services are rendered free.

7 This is another reason for doubting the decision in *Upton R.D.C. v. Powell* [1942] 1 All E.R. 220. Would not a reasonable householder, seeing a fire engine draw up outside his house and begin to put out a fire, assume the fire brigade was acting gratuitously?

8 E.g. where chattels are transferred pursuant to a contract later annulled under the rule in *Solle v. Butcher* [1950] 1 K.B. 671.

9 Assuming no intermediate mixing in a bank account, etc. See para. 10-03 ff above.

other kind of property representing my assets escapes liability provided he is innocent: it does not matter whether he gave value or not[10]).

15–07   What counts as *bona fide* purchase for these purposes? Although the matter is not beyond doubt, it seems that the concept is not limited to a purchase of the legal interest, at least as regards the first two categories above. The right to set aside a transfer for fraud[11] and (it is suggested) the equitable right to trace into proceeds are, it is submitted, best regarded as 'mere equities', which succumb to any bona fide purchaser, rather than full equitable interests good as against anyone other than equity's darling[12].

Furthermore, bona fide purchase for these purposes does not include purchase pursuant to a contract, such as a gaming contract rendered void by statute[13]. Although the matter is not settled, a transfer under a contract void for illegality, or expressed to be binding in honour only, or for value but without any contract at all[14], would no doubt be treated in the same way.

Discharge of obligation

15–08   As a normal rule, money paid (or other benefits rendered) to a person who has a legal right to receive it, and in circumstances such that the receipt discharges that right, cannot form the subject of restitutionary recovery from that person[15]. The reason is simple; whether or not the person benefiting you actually intended to do so, there is nothing unjust in your receiving and retaining what you are entitled to.

The simplest example concerns obligations as between claimant and defendant. Suppose you force me to pay you £1,000 by unlawfuly detaining my car; I can recover £1,000. Not so, however, if I already owed you £1,000 and you were merely forcing me to pay that debt: however reprehensible or even wrongful your conduct, there is (it is submitted) nothing wrong in your keeping the £1,000 and hence no injustice in your enrichment[16]. This is straightforward; but the principle equally applies where three parties are involved. In *Aiken v. Short*[17] C owed S £200, ostensibly secured on certain property of C, but in fact

---

[10] *Commercial Banking Co. of Sydney v. Mann* [1961] A.C. 1; *Lipkin Gorman v. Karpnale* [1992] 4 All E.R. 512 (claim for conversion of banker's draft representing plaintiffs' money).

[11] See *Gross v. Hillman* [1970] Ch. 445.

[12] Snell's *Equity*, 29th ed., p.25.

[13] *Lipkin Gorman v. Karpnale* [1992] 4 All E.R. 512.

[14] See the discussion at para. 10–07 above.

[15] It may, of course, engender recovery against someone else: if I am forced to pay your debt to X, I cannot recover from X but I can from you.

[16] You may, of course, be liable to me in damages for detaining the car; but that is another matter.

[17] (1856) 1 H & N 210; *cf Pan Ocean Shipping v. Creditcorp* [1993] 1 Lloyds Rep. 443.

unsecured since C was not the owner of the property concerned. A paid for the property and, with C's concurrence, paid off S; he then discovered the true facts and sought to recover from S. He failed: despite A's mistake, S had merely been receiving payment of that which was owing to him, and there was nothing unjust about his enrichment[18]. Again, suppose I engage you to do building works on my house: you induce X by fraud to act as your subcontractor in carrying them out. Although X has undoubtedly benefited me by mistake, he has (it is suggested) no cause of action against me; his act discharged your obligation to me, and it is to you that he should look for reimbursement.

One further, if obvious, point: the mere fact that an obligation exists at the time of payment will not prevent recovery if something subsequently occurs that destroys that obligation. This is particularly relevant in the case of failure of consideration. I agree to buy your car, payment due now and delivery next month, and promptly pay you £10,000. If you do not provide the car, whether owing to frustration, breach of contract or any other reason, I can recover the £10,000 even though it was technically owing at the time it was paid[19].

3 CHANGE OF POSITION

From having been an anomalous defence available in a few isolated areas of restitution[20], change of position in good faith has now become a defence of much more general application. The leading authority is the House of Lords' decision in *Lipkin Gorman v. Karpnale*[21]. Monies belonging to the plaintiffs were stolen from them by a partner and gambled at the defendants' casino. The partner's losses, predictably, much exceeded his winnings. The House of Lords, having held that the casino could not raise the defence of bona fide purchase, held that they were nevertheless protected, to the extent that they had paid out winnings to the errant partner, by a defence of change of position.

15-09

---

[18] Note, however, the effect of the rule that payment of another's debt without the debtor's concurrence does not discharge it. In such a case there is no bar to recovery from the creditor, who has not received the money in discharge of anything. See *Barclays Bank v. W.J. Simms* [1979] 3 All E.R. 522.

[19] See *Fibrosa Spolka etc. v. Fairbairn, etc.* [1943] A.C. 32, overruling the contrary heresy in *Chandler v. Webster* [1904] 1 K.B. 493. Note, however, that (inexplicably) a similar principle does not apply where the defendant is an assignee of the purchase price who is himself under no duty to provide the car: *Pan Ocean Shipping v. Creditcorp* [1993] 1 Lloyds Rep. 443.

[20] E.g. money paid by mistake to an agent who had subsequently in good faith accounted for it to his principal. These isolated instances are summed up by Lord Goff in his judgment in *Lipkin Gorman v. Karpnale* [1992] 4 All E.R. 512, 523.

[21] [1992] 4 All E.R. 512.

Obviously, change of position is only a *pro tanto* defence: if you pay me £1,000 by mistake, whereupon I give £300 to charity and spend the rest on ordinary living expenses, your claim remains good to the extent of £700.

Who can invoke change of position? The problem of 'wrongdoers'

15-10 Lord Goff in *Lipkin Gorman* suggested that change of position was a general defence, applicable to all restitutionary claims, subject to one caveat: 'it is commonly accepted', he said, 'that the defence should not be open to a wrongdoer'[22]. With respect, this is a little difficult to understand and indeed, whether such an exception is either necessary or desirable is rather doubtful. It is no doubt aimed at such unsympathetic characters as the thief, or the agent who takes a bribe, who later tries to avoid disgorging his ill-gotten gains by saying he has spent them. But such people are unlikely to be able to invoke the principle anyway, since while they have no doubt changed their position, they can hardly claim to have done so in good faith. And what about the innocent wrongdoer, such as the unwitting converter? It is hard to see why he should not have the benefit of the defence if the plaintiff chooses to waive the tort and sue for money had and received[23]. If the recipient of the plaintiff's money can claim change of position, why not the recipient of the plaintiff's goods who is sued for the amount he got for them when he re-sold them?

One further problem has already been adverted to. In *Ministry of Health v. Simpson*[24] it was said that change of position was not available as a defence to a personal claim by an executor or administrator to recover estate monies wrongly disbursed. That specific holding was referred to, but not specifically discountenanced, in *Lipkin Gorman v. Karpnale*[25]; it remains to be seen whether it remains good law.

Scope of the defence: what amounts to change of position?

15-11 On principle the defendant, to make good change of position, must show three things: (1) that having got the benefit in question he assumed

---

[22] [1992] 4 All E.R. 512, 532.

[23] True, it could be argued that he would be liable in conversion for the full value of the goods, and so to give him a defence of change of position to a restitutionary claim would be quixotic. But he may have sold the goods for more than their value; and in any case the arbitrary measure of damages in conversion is itself difficult to defend.

[24] [1951] A.C. 251. Similarly with unauthorised payments by the Crown: *Auckland Harbour Board v. R* [1924] A.C. 318.

[25] [1992] 4 All E.R. 512, 534 (Lord Goff).

he would be allowed to retain it; (2) that he had no reason to know of the possibility of his being liable to restitutionary action; and (3) action taken by him as a result of the above such that it would be unjust to make him refund. Points (1) and (2) are straightforward, and indeed are two sides of the same coin. They are neatly illlustrated by the facts of *United Overseas Bank v. Jiwani*[26] (which was in fact an estoppel case, but raised the same issues). Instructed to credit its customer's account by $11,000, a bank mistakenly did so twice. The customer immediately used the excess in part payment for a hotel. His claim that this amounted to a change of position so as to estop the bank from reclaiming its $11,000 failed; he must, said McKenna J, have had at least a suspicion that something was wrong (and in any case, his Lordship added, it was clear that he would have made the part payment from other funds in any event). Similarly, the fact that the defendant may have spent the money on ordinary living expenses is irrelevant: such expenditure cannot be argued to have been incurred in reliance on the receipt[27].

Point (3) is slightly more problematical. To begin with, it is obviously not enough merely to show that the defendant has spent money. Not only might the money have been spent anyway[28], or (as above) spent on ordinary living expenses which would otherwise have been defrayed from other funds; more importantly, it might have gone on something, such as gilt-edged stock, that is easily realisable without unreasonable prejudice to the defendant. In such a case it is hardly inequitable to continue to insist on repayment[29]. Presumably, in such cases the criterion is whether the money has gone beyond the possibility of reasonable recall by the defendant; if, and only if, it has, there will be a defence of change of position. A gift to charity is perhaps the best example[30].

15-12

A further point not touched on in *Lipkin Gorman* is how far change of position goes beyond payment of money. Transfer of property doubtless suffices: but what about more abstract reliance, such as the rendering of services? Presumably the answer must be yes; it certainly suffices for estoppel (see below), and if it did not equally work in change of position cases, the anomalies would be glaring indeed. A fraudster who has stolen £100,000 from X gives £10,000 to his son, who squanders it, and pays

---

26 [1977] 1 All E.R. 733. *Cf National Westminster Bank v. Barclays Bank International* [1974] 3 All E.R. 834. On estoppel, see below.

27 See e.g. *Lipkin Gorman v. Karpnale* [1992] 4 All E.R. 512, 534 (Lord Goff).

28 As in *Jiwani's* case, above: see too *Lipkin Gorman* [1992] 4 All E.R. 512, 534, *per* Lord Goff.

29 An example given by McKenna J in *United Overseas Bank v. Jiwani* [1977] 1 All E.R. 733, 737.

30 This also emphasises the necessity for a 'reasonableness' criterion. At least in some cases of gifts to charity, the gifts themselves might be recoverable on the ground of mistake if made on the basis of funds received by the donor; but a court would, it is suggested, be loth to require the donor in such circumstances to engage in litigation against the charity in order to repay his own transferor.

£10,000 to his counsel[31], who unsuccessfully defends him. It would be, to say the least, peculiar if nothing were recoverable from the son whereas counsel had to refund in full.

A final tricky point is whether change of position requires an act by the defendant himself, or whether any worsening in his position that can be shown to result from his enrichment ought to be in account. Take the case of the recipient of £100 paid by mistake. Granted he should not have to refund if he has spent the money in reliance, should it make any difference if the £100 has been not spent, but lost or stolen? It is submitted that it should not. The injustice to the defendant that would arise from making him repay in full is the same in both cases. Furthermore, to limit change of position to the defendant's own acts would lead to some very bizarre distinctions. It would be odd, to say the least, if my liability to repay you money I did not have, depended on whether I had handed it over to a confidence trickster (which presumably would count as spending it), or alternatively had my pocket picked in the street.

In any event, it is worth pointing out that cases where a defendant could rely on theft or loss as a defence are likely in the nature of things to be very rare: he will still have to show that the theft or loss would not have happened but for the enrichment, and this will probably be impossible except in the fairly unlikely event that, having received (say) £100 by mistake, the defendant was robbed of the very notes received before he had had a chance to bank them.

15-13   This extension of change of position has the further advantage of providing a possible solution to the problem of double liability. This concerns the fact, already mentioned in Chapter 1[32], that there is no reason on principle why the same gain in the hands of the defendant should not give rise to liability to two different plaintiffs. The sergeant in *Reading v. Att-Gen*[33], for example, could potentially have faced claims both from the Crown as his employers and from the Egyptian government as taxing authority. Again, a trustee-director who profits from his position is in the same unenviable position *vis-à-vis* both the company and the beneficiary. It is suggested, however, that in such a situation there is no reason why the handing over of the gain to one plaintiff, whether as a result of threatened legal action or otherwise, should not have the same effect as any other change of position. Once the defendant has been stripped of his illegitimate gain by one claimant, it should be regarded as unjust for him to be stripped of it again by the other

---

[31] Who does not, of course, act under a contract, and therefore by parity of reasoning with *Lipkin Gorman* cannot plead bona fide purchase.
[32] See para. 1-19 above.
[33] [1951] A.C. 507.

so as to end up out of pocket. It could then be left to the ordinary law of restitution whether the second plaintiff who thus lost out could then claim over against the first, or whether the loss would lie where it fell[34].

4 ESTOPPEL

Unlike change of position, which is not a defence to causes of action other than those based on unjustified enrichment, there is nothing peculiarly restitutionary about estoppel. Any private right, whatever its origin, may be barred by an express or implied statement denying its existence, coupled with change of position on the faith of it, in circumstances such that it would be inequitable to assert it. Nevertheless, estoppel is commonly relevant in practice to restitutionary claims, in particular where payment by mistake is concerned.

15-14

Unlike change of position, the defendant seeking to invoke estoppel needs to show a positive representation, express or implied, that restitutionary rights will not be relied on. Moreover, this is strictly applied: for instance, the mere fact that I pay you money does not, without more, carry with it a representation that you will not have to pay it back. If it did, estoppel would effectively swallow change of position in such cases. On the other hand, if I query the payment and you assure me that there is no mistake, then the matter is different: witness *Avon County Council v. Howlett*[35], where such an assurance was given to a teacher who had been overpaid and relied on by him, and as a result was held to bar the employer's action for recovery of the excess. Similarly, in *Holt v. Markham*[36] a demand for money paid by mistake was refused by the payee on apparently plausible grounds, whereupon the payer said nothing for two months and the payee spent the money. The payer was held barred by estoppel.

As for the change of position, this must obviously be on the faith of the representation; it must be *bona fide* and reasonable (i.e. without notice of the existence of a potential claim). The facts of *United Overseas Bank v. Jiwani*[37], already given, amply illustrate this. Although there is no case directly concerning restitutionary recovery, there is plenty of authority that in other kinds of estoppel, such as proprietary estoppel, reliance by act is just as efficacious as reliance by paying hard cash or transferring property.

---

[34] E.g. would the British Government in *Reading v. Att-Gen* [1951] A.C. 507, by claiming Sgt Reading's ill-gotten gains, be regarded as having adopted the sergeant's actions so as themselves to face an action by the Egyptian government? There seems no reason why not.

[35] [1983] 1 All E.R. 1073.

[36] [1923] 1 K.B. 504.

[37] [1977] 1 All E.R. 733. *Cf National Westminster Bank v. Barclays Bank International* [1974] 3 All E.R. 834. On estoppel, see below.

15-15　　　Given the availability of change of position as a defence, why plead estoppel at all, since it is in general harder to make out? There are two obvious reasons. First, the limitations on change of position, in particular, the apparent exclusion of claims arising out of wrongs, do not apply to estoppel: given a suitable representation and reliance, any claim whatever can be barred by it. Secondly, and more importantly, estoppel is unlike change of position in that it apparently operates on an 'all-or-nothing' basis, rather than merely *pro tanto*. Suppose you pay me £1,000 by mistake; you then assure me all is in order, whereupon I squander £600. If I plead change of position you recover £400: if I establish estoppel, it seems (though the matter is not absolutely certain) that you recover nothing and I get a welcome, if dubiously just, windfall of £400[38].

5 ILLEGALITY

15-16　　　The fact that I have transferred value to you pursuant to an illegal transaction does not, without more, give me a right to restitution. English law has never taken the view that payments are recoverable unless supported by good cause; hence there is no general cause of action for recovery of money – or anything else – transferred under a void contract[39].

On the other hand, there may be some additional factor besides the illegality which would normally justify restitution. I may have paid you for something you never delivered (failure of consideration): I may not have known the transaction was illegal (mistake); and so on. In such a case it has to be decided whether my right should be barred by the underlying illegality. Now, the rules on this subject are by no means clear, but broadly speaking they are as follows.

Failure of consideration: no timely repentance

15-17　　　There is no objection on principle to recovery for total failure of an illegal consideration. If I pay you £100 for a delivery of cannabis next week but change my mind next day, I can, it is suggested, recover[40]. On the other hand, once the time for performance has come and the defendant has refused to render it, then it is too late; despite the *prima facie*

---

[38] See *Avon County Council v. Howlett* [1983] 1 All E.R. 1073, leaving the point open to future argument; but the point was apparently accepted by Lord Goff in *Lipkin Gorman v. Karpnale* [1992] 4 All E.R. 512, 533.

[39] See e.g. *Scarfe v. Morgan* (1838) 4 M & W 270, 281; *Singh v. Ali* [1960] A.C. 167. Cases such as *Ingram v. Little* [1961] 1 Q.B. 31 and *Cundy v. Lindsay* (1878) 3 App. Cas. 459 may suggest the contrary; but recovery there was based on mistake, rather than on the voidness of the underlying contract *tout court*.

[40] This, at least, seems to follow from *Taylor v. Bowers* (1876) 1 Q.B.D. 291.

failure of consideration, the loss lies where it falls[41]. There are three qualifications to this, however. If the claimant (1) did not know the facts making the transaction illegal; (2) was not *in pari delicto* - i.e. substantially less morally to blame than the defendant[42]; or (3) the sole purpose of making the transaction illegal was to protect the claimant, then any right of recovery is unaffected. So, for instance, where rent control legislation forbids acceptance of advance premiums from prospective lessees, the lessee can recover monies paid by way of premium even in the absence of statutory provision to that effect[43].

Other claims

Other restitutionary claims[44] arising out of an illegal transaction will **15-18** (it is submitted) generally fail if the claimant, at the time the benefit was rendered, knew the facts making the transaction illegal. Take free acceptance and *quantum meruit*. If I perform a contract illegally I cannot claim the agreed price or any sum. If I render the same services illegally under a contract which you later repudiate, or in the unfulfilled expectation that I will conclude a contract with you in the future, the position must be the same. This is not, of course, because restitutionary claims are based on any sort of implied contract, but simply because it is against public policy that I should be able to claim payment for doing wrong. Again, take mistake. If I agree to pay you £100 to beat up X but then inadvertently pay you £200, it would (it is suggested) be very odd if I could recover the overpayment.

On the other hand, it seems pretty clear that, as with failure of consideration, a claimant not *in pari delicto*, or a claimant whom the legislation concerned was intended to protect, would have a claim even here. Suppose you agree to carry two large pieces of machinery of mine from A to B and sub-contract the work to X, who unknown to you uses a vehicle that is not licensed to carry such loads. If I wrongfully cancel the contract when one load has been carried, presumably you can sue me in *quantum meruit* for the work already done.

---

[41] E.g. *Bigos v. Bousted* [1951] 1 K.B. 92.

[42] *Cf Shelley v. Paddock* [1980] 1 All E.R. 1009 (failure to provide *quid pro quo* in contract breaching exchange control regulations). This case in fact involved a claim for damages for deceit; but it is highly likely that similar principles would apply to a claim for total failure.

[43] *Kiriri Cotton v. Dewani* (1960) A.C. 192. The basis of recovery is either duress (presumed from the provisions of the statute) or failure of consideration (the claimant has paid a capital sum for something - a lease - which the lessor was bound to provide, if at all, without such payment).

[44] We are not, of course, dealing with claims on the contract here, e.g. for the price of performance, or for damages for breach. These are not restitutionary claims, and fall to be dealt with under the general law of contract.

A particular case: restitutionary property rights

15-19   We have seen above that certain types of restitutionary rights are enforced through the manipulation of the law of property, whether legal or equitable: examples include transfers of chattels under a mistake[45]; improvements to property acquiesced in by the owner[46], conditional transfers, and the law of resulting trusts as modified by the presumption of advancement[47]. How far are these rights affected by illegality in the underlying transaction? In *Tinsley v. Milligan*[48] the House of Lords gave the answer: in so far as such proprietary rights (legal or equitable) can be established without relying explicitly on the underlying illegality, they can be enforced. Thus in *Tinsley v. Milligan* itself, a house was bought from funds belonging equally to A and B but conveyed into A's name alone to allow B to defraud the D.H.S.S. and split the proceeds with A. It was held that B could nevertheless enforce the resulting trust in her favour which arose by presumption of law. Presumably, the same result would follow if a gang of organised criminals transferred assets whose income they used to finance their activities to an ostensibly innocent third party – a resulting trust would be presumed, which could be enforced without reference to the purpose of the transfer[49]; or again, if you were to acquiesce in my making improvements to your property which, to the knowledge of both of us, you intended to use as a brothel[50]. On the other hand, this principle will not apply where the sole ground of the plaintiff's claim to the proprietary interest concerned is the illegal agreement itself. Suppose you transfer shares to your son (in favour of whom there is a presumption of advancement which neutralises any inference of a resulting trust) subject to an understanding that they are to remain yours in equity, with the object of fraudulently claiming income support. You will not be able to plead this agreement to rebut the presumption of an out-and-out gift[51].

It must be admitted that this is hardly an intellectually satisfying position for the law to take. Nevertheless, short of a general discretion in the courts to adjust property rights arising out of illegal transaction, any reconciliation of the principle *ex turpi causa non oritur actio* with the principle of security of property rights is bound to yield arbitrary answers in particular cases.

---

[45] See Chapter 3 above.

[46] *Ibid.*

[47] See Chapter 7 above.

[48] [1993] 3 All E.R. 65.

[49] Lord Goff, who dissented in *Tinsley v. Miligan*, clearly thought this followed from the decision of the majority: see [1993] 3 All E.R. 65, 79.

[50] Under the rule in *Unity Joint Stock Bank v. King* (1858) 25 Beav. 72.

[51] See e.g. *Tinker v. Tinker* [1970] P. 136 (fraud on creditors); *Chettiar v. Chettiar* [1962] A.C. 294 (evasion of land-holding restrictions). *Quaere* whether the same result would follow if the transferee executed an express trust deed: cf *Ayerst v. Jenkins* (1873) L.R. 16 Eq. 275.

6 STATUTORY BARS TO RECOVERY

In discussing illegality, we have concentrated on transactions involving wrongful – or, at the very least, immoral – activity. We now turn to the related topic of statutes that make particular contracts unenforceable: requirements of form (such as writing), provisions restricting the enforcement of contracts by those not licensed to conduct a given business, gaming contracts and the like. We know these prevent an action being brought on the contract – e.g. for sums owing, or for damages for breach. But how far do they also preclude restitutionary actions?

15–20

Restitution *prima facie* unaffected...

Although the cases do not all speak with one voice, the *prima facie* rule is that actions in restitution, being not actions on the contract but proceedings against the background of it, are unaffected by any statutory unenforceability.

15–21

Thus actions based on failure of consideration, where the claimant paid under an oral for land he never got, have succeeded despite the old s.40 of the Law of Property Act 1925 and its predecessor[52], and (it is submitted) would equally succeed under the legislation replacing it[53]. Similarly, deposits paid under gaming contracts can be recovered[54] until appropriated to losses by the payee[55] (i.e. so long as the purpose for which they were paid remains unfulfilled); and so too with premiums paid under insurance policies that, owing to lack of insurable interest, are treated as gambling transactions[56]. Similarly too, it is suggested, with mistake. Suppose you sell me Blackacre for £100,000 pursuant to an oral agreement; by mistake I pay you £120,000. Presumably I can recover the odd £20,000[57].

Again, where goods are transferred, or services rendered, under an unenforceable contract, the fact that no action will lie for any agreed price will not prevent an action in *quantum meruit* or *quantum valebat* for a reasonable sum. In practice, today such cases are likely to turn on promises to convey real property in exchange for services and similar arrangements: in the absence of any action to force conveyance of the property *in specie* (because of s.2 of the Law of Property (Miscellaneous

15–22

---

52 E.g. *Gosbell v. Archer* (1835) 2 A & E 500.

53 See now Law of Property (Miscellaneous Provisions) Act 1989, s. 2.

54 *Universal Stock Exchange v. Strachan* [1896] A.C. 166; *Re Cronmire* [1898] 2 Q.B. 383.

55 *Strachan v. Universal Stock Exchange (No. 2)* [1895] 2 Q.B. 697.

56 *Re London Commercial County Reinsurance* [1922] 2 Ch. 67.

57 But *cf Morgan v. Ashcroft*, below.

Provisions) Act 1989), the possibility of an action for the value of the services rendered may well be significant. But they could equally arise from (for instance) work done under contracts unenforceable for failure to conform to certain formal requirements. Thus in the important Australian decision in *Pavey & Matthews v. Paul*[58], the High Court was prepared to allow a restitutionary *quantum meruit* claim under a building contract otherwise unenforceable by the builder for lack of statutory formalities. It goes without saying, however, that the ultimate decision in such cases will always depend on a proper interpretation of the statute concerned[59].

... But no restitution where contrary to intent of statute

15-23 Nevertheless, if restitution would indirectly give a remedy prohibited by statute, or otherwise infringe the statutory policy, then it may be denied. Thus, if statute provides that loans to minors are irrecoverable, even where they have lied about their age, then this equally precludes the lender suing for money had and received arising out of that deceit: one cannot allow a remedy in by the back door which has been specifically excluded at the front[60]. Perhaps less defensibly, the fact that a minor cannot be held liable in breach of contract for failure to deliver goods has equally been held to preclude an action for return of a prepayment on the ground of failure of consideration[61]. Again, in *Orakpo v. Manson Investments*[62] a property developer bought a house with money borrowed from a moneylender, to whom he mortgaged it, in circumstances where statute[63] provided that the loan and any security thereunder were not enforceable. It was held that the statute equally prohibited the moneylender from being subrogated to the previous mortgages paid off with his money. On the other hand, in an Australian decision, it was held that a statutory prohibition on builders enforcing contracts that were not drawn up in due form was not intended to, and should not be held to, preclude the recovery by the builder of a reasonable sum in respect of services actually rendered[64].

---

[58] (1986) 162 C.L.R. 221.

[59] *Quaere*, for instance, whether such an order would ever be given in respect of failure by an estate agent to comply with the statutory formalities under s. 18 of the Estate Agents Act 1979.

[60] *R. Leslie v. Shiell* [1914] 3 K.B. 607. Statute now seems to allow recovery, at least where the minor still has the money: Minors' Contracts Act 1987, s. 3.

[61] *Cowen v. Nield* [1912] 2 K.B. 419.

[62] [1977] 3 All E.R. 1.

[63] The then Moneylenders Act 1927, s. 6(1) (since replaced by less draconian provisions in the Consumer Credit Act 1974.

[64] *Pavey & Matthews v. Paul* (1987) 162 C.L.R. 221.

INDEX